ANGELS

How to See, Hear and Feel Your Angels

KYLE GRAY

HAY HOUSE

Carlsbad, California • New York City • London • Sydney
Johannesburg • Vancouver • Hong Kong • New Delhi

First published and distributed in the United Kingdom by:
Hay House UK Ltd, Astley House, 33 Notting Hill Gate, London W11 3JQ
Tel: +44 (0)20 3675 2450; Fax: +44 (0)20 3675 2451
www.hayhouse.co.uk

Published and distributed in the United States of America by:
Hay House Inc., PO Box 5100, Carlsbad, CA 92018-5100
Tel: (1) 760 431 7695 or (800) 654 5126
Fax: (1) 760 431 6948 or (800) 650 5115
www.hayhouse.com

Published and distributed in Australia by:
Hay House Australia Ltd, 18/36 Ralph St, Alexandria NSW 2015
Tel: (61) 2 9669 4299; Fax: (61) 2 9669 4144
www.hayhouse.com.au

Published and distributed in the Republic of South Africa by:
Hay House SA (Pty) Ltd, PO Box 990, Witkoppen 2068
Tel/Fax: (27) 11 467 8904; www.hayhouse.co.za

Published and distributed in India by:
Hay House Publishers India, Muskaan Complex, Plot No.3, B-2,
Vasant Kunj, New Delhi 110 070
Tel: (91) 11 4176 1620; Fax: (91) 11 4176 1630; www.hayhouse.co.in

Distributed in Canada by:
Raincoast Books, 2440 Viking Way, Richmond, B.C. V6V 1N2
Tel: (1) 604 448 7100; Fax: (1) 604 270 7161; www.raincoast.com

Text © Kyle Gray, 2015

The moral rights of the author have been asserted.

The information given in this book should not be treated as a substitute for professional medical advice; always consult a medical practitioner. Any use of information in this book is at the reader's discretion and risk. Neither the author nor the publisher can be held responsible for any loss, claim or damage arising out of the use, or misuse, of the suggestions made, the failure to take medical advice or for any material on third party websites.

A catalogue record for this book is available from the British Library.

ISBN: 978-1-78180-263-2

Interior illustrations © thinkstockphotos.co.uk

Printed and bound in Great Britain by TJ International Ltd, Padstow, Cornwall

'Everything that comes from love is a miracle.'
A Course in Miracles

Contents

List of exercises

Introduction

I'll never forget the first time I physically saw my guardian angel. I was just 20 and had put all my spiritual work behind me. All the books, tarot cards and crystals had been placed into boxes and stored away.

I had been doing professional psychic readings since the age of 16 and it had been getting too much. Being recognized as the youngest medium in the UK had been exciting at first, but as the years had passed it had become more of a burden than a 'gift'.

Though I was only a teenager, I had been spending most of my time with middle-aged women or helping people with their problems. I felt as though I had a role, purpose and reason to help people, but I also felt unbalanced. I would experience the most unusual things. I'd be reading for a woman who was going through the menopause, for example, and I'd be feeling the heat! I would literally sit and have a hot flush with or even *for* her. It was not attractive! I'd also experience the most challenging of situations, from how people had passed away to the grief of those who felt left behind. I'd counsel people through their divorce. I was overwhelmed. I needed a break.

I discussed the situation with my mum and we agreed it was time to stop. I thought about going to college and my dad suggested studying music production. I went on to do so, and afterwards I worked for a while at Glasgow airport and then went on to work in a four-star hotel as an events coordinator while DJing on the side.

I loved my work in the hotel, but it definitely had its challenges. I remember about six months into the position feeling that I needed to stop bitching, blaming people and contributing to negativity. The famous quote 'Be the change you want to see' kept going through my head and I knew it was there for a reason. I wasn't the most challenging of people, but I certainly wasn't demonstrating love to the best of my ability.

I remember going to bed that night and digging out an angel book. I lay under the covers and began to read it. I got really engrossed reading about the divine beings that I had always seen, heard or felt when I was reading the cards for people. Then, as I turned one of the pages, a pure white feather fell from the book and landed on my chest. After that it was as if everything was happening in slow motion. My room lit up with the most serene golden light and more lights began to arch over my bed, looking like the outline of what I can only describe as angelic beings. I remember feeling loved, feeling safe and falling asleep knowing that we weren't the only beings in the universe...

The next morning I was woken by the alarm ringing on my phone. I was used to turning it off automatically, but that day I opened my eyes and looked at the phone. It was 7 a.m. I turned the alarm off and put the phone back on my bedside table. Then, as I looked down to the side of the bed in preparation for swinging myself out, I suddenly realized there was a man standing there looking at me. He was nearly seven foot tall and the double of Barack Obama. I shook my head, thinking I was still half-asleep, and blinked a few times. He was still there.

I felt as if I knew him, but I didn't know why. I'm not going to lie – my logical mind was thinking *What the heck is going on here?* Meantime my body just froze in awe of this magnificent being. His eyes were like fire; it was as if I was gazing into a furnace of light. And he was gazing back, just gazing into my whole being. I couldn't help but feel love. But I didn't have a clue what he wanted with me and I was late again, so I got up, went for a shower and hoped that when I got back he'd be gone.

I remember walking back into my bedroom with a towel wrapped around my waist ... and he was still there. This time I had a better look at him. He was simply standing there ... wearing armour. It was a metallic suit that fitted tightly to his body. Wow. You'd think *superhero* when you saw it.

Superhero or not, I decided that he wasn't watching me get dressed, so I did all of that in the bathroom and went to start my day.

When I got to the office that day I didn't tell anyone what I'd seen. I didn't want people to think I'd lost my mind. More importantly, what did he want with me? I knew that when things like this happened there was something more to them. I really do believe that spiritual experiences happen for a reason – and always for our greater good.

Just before lunch my mobile phone began to ring. My boss said to me, 'Will you turn that thing off?' but I was intrigued. It was a private number and I thought it could be a DJing opportunity, so I said I would take the call outside the office.

When I answered I was pleasantly surprised to hear the voice of a woman who worked for the Scottish *Sun*.

'Is this Kyle Gray the psychic?'

I replied quite abruptly, 'Well, I used to be, but not any more...'

She seemed shocked. 'What do you mean, "used to be"? Isn't this a gift? I'm calling you with regards to a new columnist position. We were wondering if you'd be interested in having an interview.'

I'm not going to lie: I wasn't interested and I definitely made my resistance clear. But after a few more phone calls and asking my mum, I decided to give in and go 'for a chat'.

So it's a week later and I'm running late (again), this time for my interview at the Scottish *Sun*.

Senior journalist Yvonne met me and settled down to ask me about my life. She was a friendly woman, in her fifties, slim and blonde, with glasses on her head that she flipped on to write and off to speak. She was interested in my work and I felt she was warm and caring. I could see her aura (the energy surrounding every living thing) sparkling and there was the light of an angel around her. As she sat there, the spirit of a cat walked in and sat on her lap. I didn't say anything, but made a mental note of it.

It was like the movie *The Devil Wears Prada* when the editor arrived. I knew he meant business and wouldn't take any nonsense from anyone.

Instantly he said, 'I've seen many of you people today. What do you read? Stones, bones, runes, graves...?'

I laughed nervously and said, 'Well, no. But I can sometimes see people's angels and I believe if we invite angels into our life we can overcome anything.'

'Oh, I quite like this,' he said, surprised, 'and I quite like you. You're young, hip and new. We've never really seen anything like it.'

That sounded encouraging, but he soon finished the interview by saying they'd be in touch. As I got ready to leave, my guardian angel prompted me to mention the cat. I remember feeling on edge and wanting to hold back, but I knew I had to prove that I was the real deal. Fortunately, it turned out that Yvonne could clearly relate to it, as her dear cat Majika had been put to sleep only days before.

I knew there was something happening here and a few days later I received an e-mail offering me a six-week position. I felt unsure, but decided to go for it. It was if I had been fighting off these angels for too long. I decided to stop fighting. To stop running away from my truth. I chose to surrender and accept the path that the angels were clearly laying out for me.

I decided to up my meditation practice and work on my skills. I went back to the hotel and told my colleagues about my experiences. They all seemed amazed. I also told them about my new job, but added that I'd continue to work there. It was my foundation at that time. Thinking about being the change I wanted to see, I decided that I'd make my work in the hotel my project. If I could be a positive role model there, I could do it anywhere.

I brought a pack of angel cards into work and laid them on my desk. I picked one every morning and allowed my colleagues to pick one too. I put positive affirmations around my desk and stuck them on my colleagues' walls as well. It was time to get positive.

Just a week later I was invited back to the Scottish *Sun* to meet some more staff members and collect a bunch of handwritten letters for my first column. To start it off, I was to read for journalists and their family and friends. Doing readings like this meant that people could see my abilities. The first column was printed on a Tuesday and it was an exciting moment.

A few days later I had a day off work and was at home when there was a knock on the door. I answered it to find the postman standing there with a huge sack.

'Have you started writing for the newspaper?' he asked.

'Yes, I have actually,' I admitted.

'Well, this is for you!' he said, handing me the sack.

I began to laugh nervously as I took it.

Then he said, 'Don't close the door, I've got another two downstairs!'

My life had changed in a week.

I remember sitting with my mum in our lounge, looking at all the letters and feeling completely astounded by the response.

'What am I going to do?' I said.

She replied calmly, with tears in her eyes, 'You'll just need to work your way through them and do your best. I'm so proud of you right now!'

After my initial six weeks at the newspaper I was given a permanent position. I continued to work at the hotel for another year, though, until in November 2011 I decided to take the leap and become a full-time spiritual consultant.

On the final day of my position at the hotel I was glad to see that everyone had worn pink as it was a Breast Cancer Relief day, and all of the senior managers had a deck of angel cards on their desk. My work here was done and my new work spreading the light of angels had truly begun.

The Obama-type being who had appeared a year earlier turned out to be my guardian angel, Kamael. He had turned up because he wanted to guide me on my path and show me my true potential to be of service to others. I listened to his call and allowed him to be my guide, and I'm so glad to be here sharing the angels' love with you today.

Welcome to the world of angels! I hope this book will help you on your journey.

Part I

WHAT ARE ANGELS?

'The angels are the dispensers and administrators of the divine beneficence towards us; they regard our safety, undertake our defence, direct our ways and exercise a constant solicitude that no evil befall us.'

JOHN CALVIN, FRENCH THEOLOGIAN

Chapter 1
Angels are real

'I'm a scientist and I believe in angels!'
DAVID R. HAMILTON PHD

Angels are an exciting subject. We all know what they are, because we've seen them on television or in the media or we've heard about them in church or from family and friends. As soon as we see a figure with a halo and wings we know it's an angel, right?

We'll also hear the word 'angel' being used to describe people who perform acts of kindness. We'll hear it being used to describe a beautiful child or a baby sleeping in their cot.

The word actually comes from the Greek *angelos*, which means 'messenger'. The 'el' comes from the Hebrew word *Elohim*, which means 'God'. Angels are messengers of God. When I speak of God, I don't mean a man with a beard and a stick, floating on a cloud, I mean the universal energy that moves through us all – an energy of love. God is love, and angels are the thoughts of God, so they are love too.

I have come to realize that we all have a guardian angel with us – a divine being, a thought of God, given to us as a gift. Our angel looks at us and falls in love. Angels love us unconditionally; they want nothing more than to help us. Their role is to support us, to guide us, to love us.

Angels are everywhere. We'll see symbols of them all around us – carved into the sides of buildings, in paintings, as a pin on our grandmother's duffle coat... We'll see that they are a reality for many people – for the religious, but also for the spiritual.

Angels are a part of most religions. In fact every belief system I'm aware of mentions some sort of spiritual presence or being either in their texts or oral tradition. The Abrahamic religions (Christianity, Judaism and Islam) all mention angels. It gets even cooler, though – Buddhism, Hinduism and Japanese Shintoism mention spiritual beings who are able to move through the air.

I grew up in a town where the majority of people were Catholic or Protestant. Growing up in a Protestant family, there was never much talk of angels. Although they were in our Bible, little attention was paid to them. When I learned later in life that the Catholic religion actually incorporates prayers to angels and speaking to your guardian angel, I really wished I'd known more about them at a younger age.

In my experience, however, angels go beyond religion. Man created religion, but God created angels. These divine beings aren't limited to a particular belief system. They are non-denominational beings who love us whether we believe in them or not.

Recently a woman contacted me after losing her partner. She had a strong belief in angels, but found it difficult to believe in God. She'd been brought up in a largely Catholic family and had felt guilty for many years about her lack of belief in God. When she began to connect with angels she felt a loving connection that she'd never experienced before. It was as if there was divine support to help her through this challenging time – support she'd never felt from what she called 'God'.

When we spoke about her situation, I came to learn that the God she'd been told about as a child was a God of fear. She'd been made aware of 'sin' and become weighed down by her mistakes and 'sins', to the point where she was now concerned about what God thought of her, frightened of the possible repercussions of her choices and even worried about whether her partner was safe in heaven.

She admitted to me that she'd avoided God like the plague, but when she'd found my work and that of other angel writers, it was if she'd come home.

I took the chance to remind her that God wasn't tied to a specific religion but was an energy of unconditional love – just like angels. I also shared with her one of my favourite quotes from the metaphysical text *A Course in Miracles*: 'God does not forgive, because he has never condemned.' That was an emotional moment, because it was then that she realized that God wasn't fear, God was love, and in some way the angels had showed up in her life to remind her of it.

If you have been brought up in a particular religion or belief system and feel guilty about not agreeing with everything it says, or you're afraid that you're going to be judged, now is the time to change. These are nothing more than illusions. The truth is that *you are loved*.

Making peace with yourself and your beliefs is one of the greatest ways to lay the foundation for a relationship with angels. Angels want you to have inner peace, and if you need to make room for it, they will help you. Always remember that you are loved and you are free. It's when you realize this that you begin to shift into a reality of love.

Take some time today to think about your beliefs and choices in life. If in your heart you have a fear of the unknown or of some sort of punishment, it's time to let it go and claim your freedom. This might not happen overnight, but it's a great opportunity to welcome in angels and let them perform their miracles.

Free will

Angels work under a spiritual law known as 'free will'. This means they can't help you until you welcome them in. That goes for the Creator too. You were sent here to make your own choices, and those choices will create waves of experience that you will go through. When you make the choice to accept help and welcome angels into your life, miracles will happen.

I'm a student of *A Course in Miracles* and it has helped me break so many boundaries in my angel work. It defines a miracle as 'a shift of perception', and so it is. It's that moment when we decide to focus on love instead of on fear. It's when we decide to forgive instead of hold a grudge.

Angels are miracle-workers. So, welcome their help and allow them to be your new role models and guides. They won't have you wearing some crazy fashion accessory, but they will change you. They'll remove the barriers around your heart and help you align with your true self – the self that loves and is loved.

Fears and old beliefs will prevent you from making a direct connection with your angels, and are both reasons why many people don't experience the angels' love and support. This is why I'm encouraging you to let go of the old and let in the love. This is why you're making room! You're clearing out the challenging stuff and making room for the loving stuff!

You've been called to this book for a reason. Probably because you're ready to make some sort of change in your life and you'd like to think there's help out there for you. Well, the good news is you've come to the right place and the exciting part of it is that there's greater support than you know just waiting to help you. Take time to soak that up.

It's now time to break down the barriers of fear and to open up to the support of the angels. They are there waiting for you right now. In fact, as you read this there are angels before you, angels behind you, angels at either side, angels above you and angels below you. Wherever you look, there is an angel just waiting to be welcomed into your life.

Believing in angels doesn't have to be a public display, by the way. It can be as private as you like. Angels don't want to bask in the limelight or be celebrities, they just want to carry out their purpose, and that is to help you and love you.

There's nothing to fear – angels won't jump out of a puff of smoke and scare you. Their energy is subtler than that. They may show you signs of their presence along the way, but the first step is more of an invitation, so that you can build up a relationship with them and truly become aware of the awesomeness that's within you.

Exercise: Welcoming help

The first step to a positive and uplifting relationship with angels is to welcome their help. For the next 10 minutes or so, ensure you won't be disturbed. Turn off the TV, close your laptop and put your iPhone on silent – it's time to connect with angels!

❖ Place your hands on your solar plexus, just above your navel, with your right hand overlapping your left, and breathe into your hands softly and deeply for a few moments to centre yourself.

❖ After a few moments of centring, open your eyes and say this prayer, either quietly to yourself or in your mind:

> *Dear angels,*
>
> *I thank you for joining me on my pathway. It is so good to know that you are real and with me. At this moment I take the opportunity to change. It is time to let go of the restrictive thoughts and beliefs that once tied me to fear and guilt. Today I choose to move in a new direction, the direction of love. Thank you, dear ones, for removing the barriers of fear from my heart so I can clearly perceive the presence of love, the presence of God and the presence of you, dear angels. I am willing to change and with positive intentions I welcome you into my life to guide me and to show me the way to a more loving, fulfilled life. I open my heart to love and accept this is the only way forward.*
>
> *Thank you, angels!*
>
> *And so it is!*

❖ Take a few moments to enjoy the space and serenity you have welcomed into your life. You may want to close your eyes and meditate in silence or write the prayer into your journal. Whatever you do, make sure you acknowledge this moment and give thanks for it before returning to your day, only now with a heart open to angelic love! Congratulations!

SUMMARY ✍

* The word 'angel' means 'messenger of God'.

* Angels are the thoughts of God.

* Angels are mentioned in different religions but go beyond religion.

* We all have a guardian angel who has been with us since birth.

* Angels love us unconditionally.

* Like angels, God is love and does not condemn.

* A miracle is a shift of perception from fear to love.

* Angels are waiting for us to invite them into our life.

Chapter 2
The purpose of angels

*'You do not walk alone. God's angels
hover near and all about.'*

A COURSE IN MIRACLES

Angels are the ultimate role models. I aspire to be like them every day. Their purpose is to guard, to guide and above all to love.

Angels are also divine healers. They're here to bring the healing rays of heaven to us. Healing doesn't have to take place on a physical level – it can be on an emotional, psychological or, even better, planetary level.

As mentioned in the previous chapter, angels can't help us, though, unless we welcome their help. They have to let us have free will. The purpose of free will is to allow us to discover that support exists for us and then to decide whether we want to be supported on our journey. We all have a reason to be on that journey and we all have lessons to go through. Angels are with us each step of the way – so now you know that, make it your business to welcome them in.

Don't expect them to remove every challenge on your path, though, because you do need to learn. We all do, and one of the things I have found out in my work with angels is that they can't always magically take us out of a challenging situation. Many of us create challenges for ourselves and angels cannot remove those challenges until we decide to make a change. But if there is something challenging going on in our life and we need to learn from it, they will guide us through it.

Empowerment

Your guardian angel knows who you really are. They see your strengths. Even when you feel low and vulnerable, they see your true potential. They see you are a source of power and they want you to realize it. So, one of their purposes is to empower you.

If there's something you're ready to let go of or a dream you're about to follow, your angel will be the wings on your back and will encourage you to take the leap.

Imagine for a moment what it would be like to have no fear. To have no doubts. To be strong, to be focused and to be filled with grace. See yourself as a bright light filled with energy, supported by the universe. This is how angels see you. It's a beautiful image to behold.

When you are ready, your angels will empower you to fulfil your purpose on this planet. All they need is an invitation.

Protection

Your guardian angel wants you to feel safe. They are dedicated to your wellbeing. Their basic function is to protect you. As I'll keep telling you, they love you more than life itself. You are treasure in their eyes, the light of their life and the purpose of their creation. They'll do everything in their power to guard you from anything that isn't serving you.

I have seen instances when people have called on angels for protection and a bright white light has wrapped around them. It's as if they're in a bubble of love and protection and away from harm.

I remember when I first discovered the power of angelic protection. It was when I was at school. I was bullied and given a hard time in my school years, especially the earlier ones, and it really affected my confidence. But when I learned about the amazing protective powers of angels, I would regularly ask them to be with me. I would imagine angels on every side of my body and know I was safe. I would also see a golden light shining around me and extending to everyone who looked in my direction. This light represented peace.

As soon as I started to put up this protective light, things changed. People instantly started being really nice to me or, even better, they just didn't bother with me at all. It allowed me to enjoy my last months of school. I ended up leaving early only because they didn't have a course in Higher Religious Studies – the one subject apart from English that I loved.

Guidance

Angels want to guide us in the right direction. They are like a spiritual GPS system. They guide us through our inner voice, but most of the time, if we aren't spiritually aware, we won't listen to it. When we begin to connect with angels, however, we are presented with a divine mapping system, internal guidance that we can use at any time.

When we ask angels to guide us, they will show us the way one step at a time. Most people, when they start to connect with angels, want to see the final outcome, but this isn't how they work. They want us to stay focused and present in our life. That's why they'll only give us one step at a time. Our job is to trust them.

Listen

Angels are brilliant listeners. Like our best friends, they'll listen without judgement. Even if we can't hear their replies, there's something so amazing about offloading onto them.

You can speak to angels out loud or internally via your mind, and rest assured they'll be listening. Even if you have thoughts that seem judgemental and negative, it's OK, your angels will listen. I have found that when we allow our frustrations to build up they become a block to inner peace, so they're definitely better out than in.

It will take some time and definitely plenty of patience for you to begin to hear your angels (more on this later), but there are other ways of interacting with them. After speaking to them about your challenges, or even what you love, you can thank them for sending you a sign of their presence, an indication that they've heard you or a hint as to what they think you should do. You'll be pleasantly surprised by what happens.

I remember a time when I was giving an angel workshop in Stratford upon Avon, the town where Shakespeare was born. It was a brilliant weekend hosted by psychic and astrologer David Wells. People from all over the UK and beyond had come to enjoy it, including a woman called Tove from Norway. She had always been spiritually minded, but hadn't spent a lot of time thinking about angels.

In one of my morning talks I introduced people to angels and encouraged them to thank the angels for reminding them of their presence. When the workshop was over we broke up for lunch. Tove met up with some friends and during the lunch break she completely forgot about requesting a reminder from the angels. But as she walked out of the front door of the hotel, a huge feather fell right at her feet. It was pure white and larger than her hand.

'People say feathers are from birds,' she said later, 'and I always agreed, but when a huge feather lands on your flipping feet with no birds in sight, you have to believe!'

It was brilliant.

When things go wrong

People often say to me, 'If angels exist, where were they when this happened...?' and tell me some sort of challenging or emotional story. My honest opinion is that angels were right there in support. Still, time and again I've heard people say, 'I believed and then this happened. If angels existed, they wouldn't let it happen.'

I completely understand that mindset. I for one don't like to hear of young children being hurt or animals treated poorly or amazing mothers coming down with a life-threatening disease. But it's important to remember that when something goes wrong here on Earth it isn't angels who choose it, it is we who choose it. When I say 'we', I'm talking about humans, our fellow brothers and sisters on this planet. Down here on Earth we feel 'pain', and we feel the heartbreak of loss, fear, challenge and separation. Angels don't believe in separation. They know that we're always with God, whatever is happening to us and whether we are in the physical body or not. Our human minds find that difficult to digest. But in heaven loss and fear don't exist. In heaven we are all one and all together, free of any darkness.

I'll never forget a woman who wrote to my column in the Scottish *Sun* about an issue that was getting to her. Margaret had been a great believer in angels all of her life and had always asked them for help. She would say a prayer to them in the morning, at lunch and before she went to bed. Though she had spent many years living on her own, she felt that she had friends and companions in her angels. She would often speak to them and call on them for support.

One night during the winter she had to go to the shops. She felt vulnerable and said to her angels, 'Please keep me safe.' Then she got her usual bus into town. When she'd picked up her shopping and got to the cash register, she noticed that her purse was missing. She knew she'd had it when she'd left because she'd taken her bus pass from it to get to town. Someone had picked her pocket.

Margaret was upset by the fact that her angels hadn't protected her belongings. 'If I do have a guardian angel,' she wrote indignantly, 'why didn't they protect me? I *did ask*, like you said!'

She had asked, but what I've found is that when we ask something of our angels from a place of fear, it isn't as effective. Margaret had said, 'Please protect me,' rather than, 'Thank you for keeping me safe.' She'd felt unsafe and then asked for help.

In fact I believe her angels probably did help her. Instead of being attacked, she had had her purse taken quietly without even knowing about it. And all of the things in it could be replaced. So, I told her to change the way she prayed, but also to see the blessing in the situation: she had been spared. She might not have her purse any more, but she did have her wellbeing!

As well as protecting us, angels want to teach us the foundation of our whole being: *love*. So, even though they can help us on a material level, they encourage us to look at the blessings in life – even in the challenging situations.

Return to light

In the conditioning of this world we've lost sight of who we are. Angels can see it, but we find it difficult. They want us to return to our natural state of being, a state where we can see, hear and feel them – because we all could once. When we were babies and children we could see both angels and those in heaven. Just look at babies now if you have any in your life. They'll laugh and smile at thin air – or is it thin air? They can see something. I believe it's angels!

We can all regain our true vision. We just have to let go first – let go of the old idea that seeing is believing. Most people on this planet will look at something and say, 'I believe it's there because I can *see* it's there.' What they're actually saying on a spiritual level is that they *only* believe in a material existence. But you see, dear friend, we are more than this – we are spirit. Our body is the home of our soul. This is the true essence of who we are. And when our physical body is ready to rest and we are ready to pass on, our body will be left behind and our spirit will soar to heaven.

The soul doesn't have eyes, but it can see; it doesn't have ears, but it can hear; it doesn't have a heart but it can feel. When we live on a more soul-based level, we can learn to see, hear and feel in a way that is beyond our human senses. This is how we experience angels.

Exercise: Seeing through the eyes of your soul

In order to reawaken this awareness, first of all you must have some faith. Trusting that there is more out there is so important for your development with the angels.

Then you must encourage your imagination to become active again. Most people believe that when you use your imagination you are 'making things up', but when you imagine as part of your spiritual development, you are encouraging yourself to see with new eyes.

Today is the day when you will learn to see differently. Encourage your imagination to see through the eyes of your soul!

❖ Sitting in your home, try to look beyond what you can see. The furniture, television and gadgets around you are on a material level of existence, but everything that truly exists is on a spiritual level. Look at your family, friends and even your pets and imagine what their soul looks like. As you do this, you may see bright colours, golds and other forms of energy swirling all around them.

❖ Imagine what it would be like to see the angels of your family, friends and pets and to connect with the true love of which we are all made.

❖ Write your impressions down in a journal, plus any ideas and awakenings you have had. This is a step towards seeing with the soul.

SUMMARY ✍

* ❖ Angels want to empower us to fulfil our purpose on this planet.

* ❖ Their role is to protect, guide and love us.

* ❖ They will always listen to us without judgement.

* ❖ Our true essence is our soul.

* ❖ We can learn to see through the eyes of our soul.

Chapter 3
How angels can help

'The angel of forgiveness takes you into the innocence again. She takes you with her, if you are ready to go.'
ROBERT HOLDEN PhD

The most beautiful thing about angels is the fact that they are absolutely desperate to help us. When they see us in distress or lost in any way, they're just waiting to be invited to bring the solution.

Angels can help us in all areas of our life. There's no aspect of life they can't deal with. As we've mentioned already, their main purpose is to love us, and with love come many different gifts, including guiding us away from fear to a place of comfort and safety.

Their main focus, though, is on something very important: the highest good. When they are supporting us and helping us with something, they will be doing it for our highest good.

For example, people often say to me, 'If you can speak to angels, can't you ask them for the lottery numbers?' Although the joke is old, I always smile. If the angels were to give me the six numbers that were going to win the lotto jackpot that weekend, what good would come from that? Sure, it might pay off my car loan and my mortgage and anything else outstanding, but what would I learn from it?

Angels know that we're here to learn, we're here to understand life and ultimately to return to love. Focusing on materialism takes us further away from love and that's not helping us in any way.

That's not to say that angels can't help us with finances or supporting our family – they can. Of course they're not going to float out of a cloud with a massive wad of cash in their hand, but they'll guide us to places and spaces where we can create abundance for ourselves, or they will get money to us that is rightfully ours.

Angels aren't all about the material world, though. They're more about the inner world. They are desperate for us to unlock the universal life-force within and discover who we truly are. As a student of *A Course in Miracles* I've learned that we are ultimately love. It's everything we are, but most of the time we don't see it. In fact it isn't something we can see, it's something we have to *know* and *trust* – just as we have to know and trust that angels are there for us.

I sat in meditation and asked for some of the aspects of life that angels can help us with and some of the gifts they are willing to offer us. Here are some of the things that came into my mind through my inner voice.

Abundance

An abundance of support is offered to us from heaven. In fact, knowing that there are angels just waiting to support us is one of the greatest gifts we'll ever receive. Take a few moments for this to penetrate your awareness.

Abundance in the spiritual sense does relate to finance too. It's our spiritual right to have enough to create a happy and comfortable life for ourselves. The key to this gift is *allowing*. It's about knowing there's enough for everyone – knowing that 'lack' is nothing but illusion.

Having said that, of course we'll look at certain places in the world and see there's 'lack' and 'desperation' there, and trust me, I know it's hard to see and deal with. Daily I see on the internet and in the media that people are dying through starvation and lack of healthcare. It is a sadness that I believe we can change. The change starts with us. Imagine if everyone thought like the angels, if everyone came from a space of love, if everyone believed – *knew* – that there was plenty for all, then there wouldn't be hunger, starvation and lack in the world, there would be an abundance of sharing, love and care.

One of my greatest beliefs is that when we share, we receive. According to *A Course in Miracles*, 'It is as blessed to give as to receive,' and I really believe that's true. When we share, it's our way of saying, both internally and to the universe, 'I know there's enough to cover what I'm giving and sharing today.' And the universe hears what we say. The divine angels of abundance shine their light around us and more material support is brought to us. It's the law of cause and effect. So, let's all be the change and share today. If we give selflessly, without holding back, we will receive.

A prayer for receiving

Thank you, angels of abundance, for blessing my life with your presence and support.

I know there is plenty in the universe for us all.

I choose to receive what I deserve and share my gifts with the world in any way I can!

And so it is!

Happiness

Happiness is our function. It's the one thing most of us are really looking for. We want to be at peace, we want to feel comfortable, we want to enjoy life.

I've found that not only do angels offer us the gift of happiness but they're attracted to us when we express it! They love to see us smile and laugh. They love high energy and are attracted to it like iron filings to a magnet. When we are low or depressed, on the other hand, a cloud gets in the way of our connection to the angels.

So, if you are feeling lonely and unsupported, watch something funny, be around friends who make you smile, do something fun! When we laugh and express joy, angels will join us.

A Course in Miracles says, 'Be happy, for your only function here is happiness,' and it's true. When we lose sight of happiness, we lose our true function: to be a bringer of joy.

I really believe that's why I love music so much. When I listen to it, I feel as though I'm lighting up. I'm ecstatic and I turn into a huge radio transmitter, beaming out happiness and joy. And angels respond. I've danced with friends in nightclubs to my favourite DJs and seen angels all around us. As we cut shapes and move to our favourite beats with joy in our hearts, angels encircle us. They watch us loving life and they join the party.

Invite your angels in today and thank them for being present on your love train. Thank them for bringing you the joy of life and hooking you up with your divine and only function: to be happy and express happiness. When you send out your intention, it will be heard. Prepare to laugh!

A prayer for happiness

Thank you, angels of happiness and joy, for lighting up my life with your presence so that I can express my true function: to be happy!

Today I take the time to express my joy and recognize I will attract more and more!

And so it is!

Harmony

Angels can help end conflict and bring peace. When a situation gets heated and negative, we lose touch with our true essence. Then it's as though a shell of fear is created which blocks angels from getting in. When they're invited in, however, their rays of love and healing wash over the situation, breaking the shell and reminding us all of who we truly are: *love*.

Most of the time, conflict arises from our fear and our selfishness. It is created when we see something in a different way from another person. We try to get our point across, but often don't succeed. Communication breaks down, anger sets in, grievances take place and love is forgotten.

In this state, we can end up asking ourselves many questions, especially when we feel we're hitting a brick wall, everything from 'Do they understand my point?' to 'Why can't they see how I feel?'

My favourite question comes from *A Course in Miracles*: 'Would you rather be right or happy?' I certainly know the answer to that one!

Angels encourage us to stop fighting, to stand down in the heat of the moment and to take ourselves away from the conflict. Sure, they tell us to stand up for our beliefs, but in the heat of an argument we'll never get through. We have to do it another way.

We can call on angels to bring harmony and peace to a situation of course, but when we do that we have to trust, we have to believe, we have to *surrender*. When we surrender, we take a step back and *allow* the divine to take its course. We allow the angels to perform their duties and miracles.

The one thing that angels are dedicated to is fairness. They won't ensure we 'win' an argument, but they will bring in harmony, peace and fairness so that we can all move on with our lives.

If we feel that someone should be punished for something, or pay a karmic debt, then we are unfortunately coming from the wrong space. When someone is doing something harmful or something we don't like, they are coming from a space of fear, so we must bless them and pray for their return to love. If we want negative things to happen to them then we too are far from being our true self.

A prayer for harmony

Thank you, dear angels, for surrounding my home, family, relationships and career in your harmonious light so that I can live to my full potential!

For a specific situation you can say:

Thank you, angels, for surrounding me, this situation and everyone involved in love and harmony so that we can find a peaceful solution.

I surrender this to you, knowing you will lead the way.

And so it is!

Forgiveness

Forgiveness is the key to all our challenges. It is a bridge to a deeper awareness of the divine and ultimately ourselves. When we don't forgive, we allow toxicity to build up in the core of our being and resentment will begin to grow. Resentment is a huge barrier, it's like the Great Wall of China, and we can't see over it. This huge wall stands between us and love.

When we find it difficult to forgive, we are seeing ourselves as separate from God. We are never separate from God, but resentment can make us think so.

If you find forgiveness challenging, angels can help you. These divine beings will help you see through their eyes – and they never hold any grievances.

Most people avoid forgiveness because they feel it means they're letting someone get away with bad behaviour. But according to the angels, forgiveness is an act of self-love, because when we forgive another person, or even ourselves, we let go of resentment and toxic thoughts, and these thoughts and feelings can cause more problems than we can even imagine. It's time to see the truth.

When I started to work with angels I was stubborn, and 11 years later I'm still stubborn, but I have learned the value of forgiveness. I didn't really understand what forgiveness was at first, but I knew it needed to take place. It has allowed me to see clearly, it has allowed me to experience life and it has opened the doors to peace.

The angels are encouraging you now to let go of your shoulda, woulda, coulda thoughts. It's time to let fear out and love in. It's time to forgive.

Even if you don't know how to forgive, you can ask the angels to show you how. All you need is the willingness to forgive and they'll be with you every step of the way. Just think about it: would you rather have the toxicity of challenges or the freedom that forgiveness brings? Now is the time!

A prayer to bring forgiveness

Dear angels of forgiveness,

I thank you for joining me on my journey.

I am ready and willing to release all that is no longer serving me.

It is time I claimed the peace I deserve in my life. I am willing to forgive.

I know that it's not always been easy for me to do so in the past, but now I'm ready to change.

Thank you for showing me the miracle of forgiveness and for lighting my path towards it! I surrender!

And so it is!

Exercise: Forgiveness

❖ Take some time to think about the gifts that angels have to offer. Are there any areas of your life where you would like their help? If so, welcome them in. Thank them in your own way for shining the light of their presence on the people, place or situation and allow them to help.

❖ Are you feeling that an area of your life is blocked?

❖ Ask yourself this very important question: 'Who do I need to forgive?'

❖ The first person that comes into your mind is the person the angels are encouraging you to forgive. Take time to send them love. You can do this by imagining them surrounded in a pink healing light. Once you have done this, you can tell them in your mind that you have set them free, that you have forgiven them (and that person can be you, too).

❖ Then use the prayer on page 37 to work the miracle of forgiveness.

SUMMARY

❖ Abundance is our spiritual right.

❖ Joy and happiness are our only function.

❖ Laughter and smiles act as a magnet for angelic presence.

❖ Angels bring fairness and harmony to conflict.

❖ Forgiveness removes the blocks on the way to peace and purpose.

Chapter 4
Choirs of angels

*'Angels are pure thoughts,
winged with truth and love.'*
MARY BAKER EDDY, FOUNDER OF CHRISTIAN SCIENCE

There are billions of angels, so many I couldn't even count them. There are more angels than there are people and animals put together – this I know for sure, because we all have a guardian angel. Our guardian angel is our divine gift from God and is with us right now – it's so exciting!

There are many different types of angel, just as there are different races of people, but they are all ultimately one. All of them are love, all of them are peace and all of them are working for the source of our creation.

The angelic hierarchy

There are different ideas on the hierarchy of angels. Many people have attempted to understand and explain it, and I am one of them of course, but we can never be entirely sure of the details. There is only so much the human mind can comprehend, especially in regard to God. We can, however, develop our personal connection to angels in the hope that we will become closer to them and gain a true understanding of their qualities and power.

The hierarchy that I have always connected with comes from Catholic texts. I haven't followed it word for word, though. In fact, when I was writing my book *Angel Prayers*, I meditated on each type of angel to ensure I was sharing the best information I could.

When it comes to understanding angels better, sometimes it's good just to know their rank and how they are said to work. So, here's the hierarchy:

Spheres

The hierarchy of angels is broken down into three tiers known as spheres. Each sphere contains three different types of angel. Angels of a particular type are known as a choir. So, to make things easy, there are nine choirs of angels, organized in three spheres.

Each choir of angels has an overall purpose, though there will be angels in each choir that have special gifts to offer. All angels have one true focus, though: love and peace for the whole universe.

We will probably only work with two or three types of angel in our existence on Earth. The reason for that is some of their roles will go beyond what we can be involved with while we are here. I do, however, feel it's good to know who's up there and working for love.

The way I like to explain the spheres of angels is that they all stand around the heart of God. In the centre of the spheres is the energy of God, and that energy is sending out thoughts. These thoughts create angels. The angels look back at God and sing his praises and the praises of all of his creation. They are a creation of God's love, so wherever they go, they radiate this energy.

The first sphere

Seraphim
The Seraphim are the highest choir of angels. Seraphim means 'burning ones' and these angels are beautiful flames of universal love. Many texts say they have six wings. If angels had a government, it would be the Seraphim. Known for their beautiful singing, they sing the praises of God, bringing energetic shifts and waves of healing to the whole universe.

Cherubim
This is the choir of angels that created the idea of 'cherubs'. These divine angels are so knowledgeable about the universe. In fact their name means 'fullness of knowledge'. They are God's record-keepers. They are closely connected with the Akashic Records – a chronicle of every event that has ever happened in the whole of creation.

Thrones

These angels have been seen as wheels of light. The word 'Throne' relates to the seat on which God actually sits. Although God goes far beyond a man actually sitting on a seat, these angels are close to the source of all of creation. They are in control of the shifts of consciousness in the universe. I truly believe they are working closely with planet Earth right now as we move into a greater awareness of spirit and love.

The second sphere

Dominions

Dominions regulate the role of every angel apart from those in the first sphere. Their name means 'lordships' and they have a real sense of authority. These are the angelic beings who oversee international affairs. They are wonderful to call on for help in international situations, including conflicts and disasters.

Virtues

Virtues are the angels who look after the flow of nature. They ensure that the world is balanced according to the natural laws and bring blessings to individual countries. The name means 'strongholds' and I truly believe these angels weave the natural flow of the life-force.

Powers

Powers are the race of angels that encourages us to remember there is a better way. Their whole purpose is to try to end conflict, destruction and war. They are made of pure compassion and they send waves of their light to the world, especially to those who are trying to push the destruct button on our beautiful planet and people. They can protect us when we call on them, especially if we are asking them to support us on a national level.

The third sphere

Principalities

These are the angels who protect spirituality, including spiritual texts. Their name means 'rulers' and they have a strong connection with the world leaders and activists who want to make this world a better place. These angels help reveal spiritual truths in science so that we can understand the divinity of our creation even more.

Archangels

Archangels are the 'boss angels'. They're the 'managers' in charge of all of the guardian angels who look after Earth, its inhabitants and their journey of spiritual growth. Archangels are a magnificent group of angels and are ready and willing to work with us at any time. I like to look at them as phenomenal celeb-type angels. Everyone knows who they are in heaven and knows their amazing gifts and talents. There are thousands of archangels, but some are better known to us than others. In Chapter 7 I introduce you to the four major archangels and suggest ways in which you can connect with them.

Angels

The final choir of angels is the most exciting. This includes our own very dear guardian angels, the healing angels and the angels of planet Earth. This is the choir that we have direct access to when we tune in to angels. They are what this book is all about. When we send our thoughts to heaven, the angel who is best able to help us will leave this choir and come directly to us. If they feel they will need the support of a higher angel, they will go to them and they will do the work together. It's a beautiful thought.

When I speak to heaven, I always say 'angels' in the general sense, because I know that there are so many out there and that the angel who can help me best will come to me. However, you can address a particular angel if you know them by name or you can just focus on that angel and they will hear you. Whatever works for you will be right for you.

Exercise: Calling on angels

Now that we've learned about all of the amazing angels out there in the universe, it's only fair that we acknowledge their presence. Here's a prayer I've written to call on these amazing beings. I invite you to take some time to think about life, then light a candle and meditate on world peace for a while before calling on angels with the following words:

> *Mighty Seraphim,*
> *Singers of God's love,*
> *Blessed Cherubim,*
> *Keepers of knowledge from up above,*
> *Thrones of light,*
> *I call on you now.*
> *Your support and harmony I allow.*
>
> *Dominions, Virtues and Powers,*
> *Bring world peace.*
> *Principalities and Archangels,*
> *Guide me as I release.*
>
> *Thank you, dear angels, for blessing me.*
> *May you protect me in air, on land and on sea.*
> *I am one with all that is.*
> *Universal blessings,*
> *I commit to this.*
>
> *And so it is,*
> *So mote it be,*
> *God's grace has blessed me,*
> *And I am free.*

SUMMARY ✍️

- ❖ Angels are waves of God's thought.

- ❖ There are nine choirs of angels, organized in three spheres.

- ❖ Each choir of angels has an overall purpose.

- ❖ All angels have one true focus: love and peace for the whole universe.

- ❖ We will probably only work with two or three types of angel in our existence on Earth.

- ❖ When we call on angels in general, the one who can help most will come to us.

Chapter 5
Guardian angels

*'You're in the arms of the angel, may
you find some comfort there.'*
SARAH MCLACHLAN, MUSICIAN AND SINGER

Your guardian angel is the best gift you've ever been given. They'll always look after you. They're standing by your side right now, pouring their love into you. When you learn more about them, you'll realize that they've loved you unconditionally since the time of your creation.

In previous books and when I've spoken about angels, to make things easy I've said our guardian angel is given to us at birth. But the real truth of the matter is we connect with our angel before we come to Earth. Our soul knows our guardian angel. I like to think of the soul and the angel as best buds. They're in constant communication with each other, they don't like to lose sight of each other and they're connected through love. So, even if you haven't connected with your guardian angel so far in this life, you'll already know them.

When you do connect with your guardian angel, it's like coming home. They remind you of the things you've forgotten and the purpose of your life. They are your protector and your guide.

'Speaking' to your guardian angel

You can speak to your guardian angel and they can speak to you. They'll do this through your intuition and spiritual senses. Their energy is subtle, so their communication won't be in your face, but if you're alert and prepared for it to happen, you'll begin to feel their frequency.

Beyond words

Our guardian angel speaks to us in a way that goes beyond words. Yes, they can send us voice snippets, but their communication is usually via energetic waves. So instead of hearing them say something, we might just have a sense of knowing something without explanation.

For instance, have you ever just woken up with the feeling that you're not supposed to drive home a certain way, only to hear later that there were delays or even a huge accident on that road? Your angel probably sent a message to you, because their job is to protect you.

Finding feathers

Your guardian angel will often send you a sign of their presence. Once of the best ways of doing this is sending you a little feather. There's something really positive about finding a feather on your path – it's a wee reminder that you are loved and protected. Of course, it's only natural to find feathers where there are birds or feathered pillows, etc., but when you find a feather in a place where there is no logical explanation for it then you know it's the work of an angel.

My mum often receives feathers from her guardian angel. They just appear out of thin air. It's quite amazing. One time she was going to work and had to do some errands on the way. She took the car to save time, but after her final errand she was worried she was going to be late for work, and if anyone knows my mum, they'll know she likes to be on time. When she got back in the car, sat down and prepared to drive off, a feather fell from the roof of the car and landed on the passenger seat beside her. She knew then that all was well and that she'd be on time that day.

I've had so many different feather experiences! I remember when I'd just signed my first book deal and was going to meet my friends in the pub to tell them the good news, I called a cab and decided to go outside and wait for it as it was a beautiful summer's evening. As I stood there waiting for it to arrive, a feather fell out of the sky and I put out my hand and it landed directly in it. It was like something out of a movie. Every hair on my body stood on end.

Desperate for a sign?

It's always lovely to receive a sign, but I always say to people that being desperate for a sign isn't going to help them. I believe signs are brought to us when we already have faith in angels. When we rely on signs to prove the existence of love, we truly aren't coming from the same place.

Of course angels often send us signs when we're low or need a reminder that there's help out there. But they don't want us to rely on signs, because that's bringing our focus to the external and the physical. True love is an *internal* journey – that's why we have to have faith in the angels, because faith goes beyond what we can see. When we understand this, we create a sense of oneness with heaven.

You can use the following prayer to ask angels to send you a sign of their presence, but know that it'll only be sent when you really trust that they are there.

A prayer for a sign

Thank you, angels, for sending me a sign of your loving presence in my life.

It's so good to know you are with me each step of the way!

Divine timing

Angels teach us that everything happens according to divine timing. That is, everything happens at a specific time for a specific reason. Accordingly, they teach us to be patient and to trust.

Remember that angels can help us in the material world but they don't encourage materialism. So if, for example, you want them to help you get your dream car or dream job, they probably can, but their hope is that you'll see the blessings you already have in your life first. If you're pulled into a materialistic whirl of wanting, there's a good chance they'll make you wait or not help you move on because you have to find the blessings in your current space.

Divine timing works in other ways too. It may not be obvious. We all know people who passed on too young and it may be difficult to believe that it happened for a good reason. But angels know where we go when we 'die', and it's a place filled with love. If we remember this, it can ease the pain we feel.

On the other hand, angels can save a person's life if it's not their time to go. I expect you've heard stories of angelic rescue – an unseen presence pulling a person back onto the pavement in time to save them from being hit by a car, or a voice telling someone about to commit suicide to stop. You may even have experienced something like this in your own life.

We've already learned that angels can't help us unless we ask them, though, so how does that work? I've learned there is a little sub-clause in that rule. Angels can step in and help us if we've reached a state of despair and are about to make a decision that will ultimately prevent us from fulfilling our purpose. You see, our ego mind can take over the show and push us into a dark hole of existence. In there we can lose all sense of love and fail to see the light waiting to guide us. Yet at the same time our soul can be sending out a huge SOS signal to heaven. If it's part of the divine plan then angels can come in and take us to safety.

There's no dark night of the soul; it's always light. There is a dark night of the *ego*, but in the end angels can override the ego's voice, especially if the universe has asked for that to happen.

It's the same with near-death experiences: angels can intervene if it isn't your time to go. If, say, before this life you decided to become a wonderful healer for our planet or a true leader devoted to peace and at one point you were about to die, they would help you avoid it so you could fulfil your purpose. In most cases, the experience itself would prompt you to do so.

Animals and angels

If we all have a guardian angel, do animals have them too? Many people wonder about this and I've found that the animal kingdom does have angels watching over it.

The angels of animals are beings I like to call 'elementals'. They're slightly different from guardian angels, more suited to nature and the elements. They're dedicated to the Earth and its inhabitants.

However, we can ask angels to support the animal world. If we know of an animal going through some sort of trauma or in need of healing, we can speak to our own guardian angels and ask them to help.

I've chosen to be vegetarian in this lifetime because I've come to realize that animals have souls too. When I see someone's dog respond to them or I call my Siamese cat, Ralph, and he comes bursting into the room with meows and purrs, there's no denying these beings have souls.

Just like us, when they 'die', animal souls go to heaven. They are released from the Earth to rejoin the energy of love that I like to call God or the universe. All souls are eternal and all souls are connected to this source. Angels are a creation of this source, so naturally they can protect not just human souls, but other types of soul too.

Exercise: 'Dear guardian angel...'

A wonderful way to connect with your guardian angel is to write them a letter. They've been with you through every up and every down and it's always wonderful to take the opportunity to acknowledge them.

❖ It may not have been easy to get to the point you're at now and your guardian angel may have helped you through many challenges. Think of times of hurt, illness, emotional difficulty, feelings of being alone... You weren't alone – your angel was there. Take some time to write them a letter to tell them how thankful you are to have reached this point on your journey and to have realized that they are with you now. Thank them for any synchronistic events or signs you have received that could be due to them and thank them for where you are today. If there's anything else you feel is important to share with your angel, now is the time. Think of them as an amazing counsellor and know that they'll read your letter without judgement. How miraculous is that?

♦ When you've completed your letter, put it into an envelope and seal it. You can keep it at the back of your journal or in a special place. Many people like to burn their letter as a symbol of transformation. Do what feels right for you.

SUMMARY ✍️

♦ Our guardian angel is always looking after us.

♦ Angels teach us that everything happens according to divine timing.

♦ Angels can save us if it's not our time to go.

♦ Angels can speak to us in ways beyond words.

♦ Feathers are signs of angels' presence.

♦ Animals are protected too, by elementals, and we can call on our angels to help animals.

Part II
WORKING WITH ANGELS

'Our guardian angels are our most faithful friends, because they are with us day and night, always and everywhere.'
ST JOHN VIANNEY

Chapter 6
Meeting your guardian angel

'God made us angels of energy, encased
in solids – currents of life dazzling
through a material bulb of flesh.'

PARAMAHANSA YOGANANDA, YOGI AND GURU

It has now come to the point where you know enough about angels to meet your very own guardian angel. This is the most exciting part of spiritual development in my eyes. Together with your guardian angel, you can open doors and benefit from opportunities to have a more abundant, loving and support-filled life.

Your angel's appearance

Angels are pure beings without physical form. They are ultimately the energy of the universe, the divine thoughts of the Creator. So your guardian angel will show themselves to you in a way that you will understand.

I have seen angels in many forms. Sometimes I'll be doing a reading for someone and I'll see a beautiful tall woman in a flowing gown with bright golden locks to her waist. The typical Hollywood angel, you may think. Well, that's absolutely right. Angels will take the idea you have in your mind and embody it so that you can understand them.

My guardian angel, as you already know, is the double of Barack Obama. I'm not entirely sure why, but that's the form he has chosen to show himself in. He wears armour, like a warrior. He is strong and courageous. The thing that surprises me most about him is his eyes – they are swirls of purple and flickering orange flames. I have seen him with wings and without them. He doesn't smile with his mouth, he smiles from his heart. Every time I look at him I feel safe and loved and know that I'm not alone.

I regularly host angel workshops all over. Recently, while hosting one in Scotland, I opened the day with a meditation to meet your guardian angel. I told everyone that there was no rush with this process and if nothing came through then that was fine, but if they got something, even better. I always encourage people to have an open mind, but without the expectation that something is just going to pop out.

I led the group, which was sitting in a circle, into a deeply relaxed state. In this state we visualized ourselves in a golden light of protection and safety before going to an imaginary cave on a beach. Inside the beautiful amethyst-filled cave I encouraged the group to imagine a bench to sit upon. 'On that bench, waiting for you, is your guardian angel,' I said, before going on to add, 'spend some time with them and make a mental note of their looks, their height, how they feel and if they reveal their name to you.'

After the exercise, the group shared their experiences. One girl's really amazed me. She got to the bench in her meditation to find a blue geometric triangle floating in the air. It lit up and gave off a feeling of ultimate love and acceptance. When she asked in her head, 'Are you my angel?' it answered, 'Yes!' Then it enveloped her in an amazing shimmering blue light of protection and healing.

After the meditation we talked and it turned out that she had a blue geometric triangle pendant on and this was a familiar image to her – she loved triangles. For her, a blue triangle felt safe, comfortable and balanced.

You see, angels want you to feel comfortable in their energy and will present themselves as whatever makes you feel safe. They will adapt to you!

Your guardian angel's name

It's lovely to know the name of your guardian angel, but it's not important. Names are something we usually focus on a lot because on the material level of existence everything has a label. But angels are energy, pure energy, and work on vibration, so it is intention that works for them. So even if you know you guardian angel's name, it won't improve your connection with them. If you want to know how to get your angel's name see page 66, but again, don't worry if you can't get it.

The name of my angel came to me very clearly when I first did a meditation to meet him. I heard a voice and I heard his name, but that was all I got. Nothing else came through for years. One day I woke up and it all just clicked into place, but for years I asked and asked and asked to no avail.

Developing a connection with your guardian angel doesn't happen overnight, but don't be discouraged – it's an experience to be savoured.

Your angel's voice

You can learn to tap into the voice of your angel. For many years I heard my angel speak to me in the sound of my own voice. In times gone by I also heard a very well-spoken, almost upper-class English voice, which was always very direct and to the point.

In this respect, too, your angel will adapt to you and will mostly speak to you in a way you know. For most people that is through the 'inner voice'. The inner voice is a voice you'll know very well. You'll use it when you're speaking internally to yourself, when you're thinking about your shopping list, your plans for the day, what you need to do next... It's the voice that you use to say prayers and speak to your angels.

The challenge here is that the inner voice can sound very similar to the ego. The ego will even use the inner voice against you. It'll sound very similar and it'll tell you challenging things. So, for example, you'll look in the mirror and feel quite good about yourself and all of a sudden this voice that sounds like your own will say, 'You look fat,' or, 'Have you seen how bumpy your skin is today?' or something else that's cheeky and quite uncalled-for.

Our task is to quieten this voice so we can tap into our guidance. This will take practice, and most importantly patience, but if we're disciplined enough, we'll do it. And once we've learned to differentiate between the voice of divine guidance (God and the angels) and the voice of our ego (the internal doubt system) we'll experience real growth.

Having said this, many people do have the natural gift of hearing their angel's voice clearly. In most cases that's because it's so different from their own inner voice. If you're one of these people, congratulations on this magnificent gift you have received. If you aren't – don't worry, it'll come! Believe!

To help you understand the difference between the two voices, here are some bullet points.

The voice of your angel will be:

✦ loving

✦ guiding

✦ reassuring

✦ strong

✦ direct

 ❖ encouraging

 ❖ safe

The voice of your ego will sound:

 ❖ distracted

 ❖ uncertain

 ❖ negative

 ❖ vindictive

 ❖ critical

 ❖ discouraging

 ❖ needy

Emotional experience

Connecting with angels can be not only exhilarating, but very emotional too. I'll never forget the time I was conducting an angel meditation to an audience of over 1,000 people in Austria. I was super-excited to be in town, as on my previous trip to Austria my flight had been cancelled and I'd had to conduct my talk via the internet.

I remember speaking to the event organizer that day and agreeing that I wouldn't use my PowerPoint presentation on the angels but just speak from the heart. I'd one goal that day and that was to help at least one person meet their angel. If I can do that per event, or even just make someone feel safe, I really believe I've done my job.

I was so comfortable in the room that day that I sat on the end of the stage with my feet dangling off the side. After talking about my life and work, I invited the audience to join me in a prayer and meditation. As I went through the meditation, I closed my eyes and could feel the centre of my chest pulsating. The love in the room was overwhelming. I could feel my adrenaline building, my eyes beginning to fill up and unconditional love enveloping my whole body.

I opened my eyes to ensure the audience was OK and as I looked up I could see angels everywhere, hovering above everyone in the audience. Some were pouring their light into the tops of people's heads while others were embracing people or placing their hands on their shoulders.

I remember saying, 'Your angels are with you right now. All around you. In front, behind and to either side angels are present. This is a gift. Feel and accept it today!'

At the same time a translator was relaying my words to the people who couldn't speak English.

All of a sudden, people just began to cry. Hundreds of people were brought to tears that day. The love in the room was magnificent. We all felt it. I remember thinking, *Wow, this is a true gift*, as I looked out at a sea of grown men and woman crying and feeling the love of the angels all around them.

I really believe that when we truly feel the love of angels we will cry – we'll share emotion and we'll let it all out.

The love of angels is unconditional in ways that words cannot express. It's a divine energy with unlimited love and acceptance. It truly is miraculous.

Speaking to your angel

You don't need to have any formal conversation with your angel. It's fine if you just chat away to them in your head, or even out loud if you're comfortable doing so. I often just gab away to my angels. I love doing it. I'll just tell them what's on my mind (even though they probably can see it) and I'll trust there's someone listening. Often I'll hear a reply. Not always, but there's something really comforting about it. Angels don't need formality; they enjoy the fact that you're comfortable speaking to them just like the true non-judgemental friends they are.

I often speak and pray to my angels while on the move. I've even been known to do it out loud. I was caught by a woman once in a supermarket. She smiled in my direction and I honestly don't mind people knowing. I was caught off-guard recently, though, while walking through Glasgow Central train station. I walk through the station every day, as it's a shortcut from where I park my car to my office block, plus I usually grab lunch from Marks and Spencer on my way through. I was just coming through the station and about to go up the escalator while saying, 'Oh, it's so good to know you're here with me, angels. Thanks for making today so positive and exciting,' when I bumped into my friend Caragh. She smiled and said, 'You really do speak to them, don't you?!' There was no denying it – I do!

Issued

Branch: Millennium Library
Date: 02/09/2021   **Time:**   11:53 AM

ITEM(S)   **DUE DATE**

Angels : how to see, hear and...   23 Sep 2021
30129076924068

Your current loan(s): 3
Your current reservation(s): 0
Your current active request(s): 0

To renew your items please log into 'My
Account' on the library website
norfolk.spydus.co.uk

Thank you for using your local library.

Current Transactions

Branch: Millennium Library
Date: 02/09/2021   **Time:** 11:53 AM

ON LOAN	DUE DATE
The power of the soul : [paperb... 30129076477034	23 Sep 2021
Untying the karmic knot : [pap... 30129078326197	23 Sep 2021
Angels : how to see, hear and ... 30129076924068	23 Sep 2021

Speaking to angels instead of God

Many people who come from a religious background will say to me something like 'Isn't it wrong to speak to angels instead of going direct to God?' When I hear this it tells me this person is afraid of offending God. But angels are the thoughts of God, they are his creation and they were created to guide us. What would be the point of their existence if we didn't communicate with them?

God doesn't feel bad about it, because God is the love source that extended energy to create the angels and, of course, us. When we speak to angels we're acknowledging God by speaking to the guiding energy he provided for us. That's why it's great to speak to angels.

Praying to your guardian angel

You can speak to your guardian angel through prayer. This is something I love doing. I have some prayers I repeat daily or for specific requests. I like ritual and I like doing something often, as it really sets the intention. Daily I'll wake up and say a prayer to God and the angels and before I hit bed in the evening I'll close the day with a prayer too.

It actually took me some years to master my prayers. I learned to pray through going to Sunday school and the Boys' Brigade, and I loved my time in both. They both taught that you could ask for help and that if you had faith, your prayers might be answered. So from very early on I'd put my requests to God and I'd hope that the future would deliver my answer. Over the years some prayers were answered and others weren't (or so I thought).

Since then I've dabbled with many different approaches and a breakthrough came when I learned something really important: help is already here. Yes, help is already present. God and his angels are just waiting to help us and they're waiting *for us to turn up*. It is our job to accept the help that is already there for us.

So, instead of saying 'Please, angels, please, God' in my prayers, I decided to say 'Thank you, God and angels' as a way of acknowledging the help I truly believed was already present. I spoke as if my prayer had already been answered and I trusted that it had been heard and was being dealt with by the divine. Since then I've never failed to be amazed by the answers to my prayers.

There is a selection of affirmations and prayers at the end of this book (*see page 167*). For now, why not try connecting with your guardian angel via a meditation? This is the key to creating a wonderful bond with your angel.

Exercise: Guardian angel meditation

When I first learned to meditate I'd often record my own voice talking myself through the steps of a suggested meditation so that I could really relax without having to open my eyes and look at the next step. Most mobile phones have the resources to do that, but if that's challenging for you, why not work with a partner who can take you through the steps and then you can do it for them?

The key to a good meditation is being able to relax, so that means breathing nice and deeply through your nostrils while sitting upright either in a cross-legged position on the floor or with your back straight in a chair with both feet on the floor. Are you in that position now?

❖ Close your eyes.

❖ Breathe gently in and out of your nostrils and focus on your breath. Don't force yourself to breathe deeply but allow yourself to breathe in a way that feels right for you.

❖ Visualize a golden light washing over the crown of your head and moving to cover your whole body, right down to the tips of your fingers and toes.

❖ Say 'Thank you, guardian angel, for joining me in this space and for revealing yourself to me.'

❖ In your mind, become aware of your angel standing before you.

❖ The angel stands there in all of their glory. Become aware of how they look to you.

❖ First, see the angel's aura. Note the colour of this light.

❖ Then see their face forming in front of you. Become aware of their features.

❖ See the angel's hair. See their dress. See their wings.

❖ In your mind say, 'Thank you for revealing your name to me.' Trust the first name the angel gives you.

❖ The next thing you can do is ask your angel some questions or speak to them about anything on your mind.

❖ Take some time to enjoy their company. Feel their embrace and hug them back. See the unconditional love they hold for you. They are with you now.

❖ When you've finished your meditation; thank them and open your eyes!

Make a note of your experience in a journal so you can add to it as you go on.

SUMMARY ✍️

❖ Your guardian angel doesn't need formalities to speak to you.

❖ Your angel will speak to you in a way you understand.

❖ Knowing your angel's name isn't important.

❖ God encourages you to speak to your angel.

❖ Every prayer is heard by angels.

❖ Help is already present, so give thanks for it in your prayers.

Chapter 7

The power of archangels

'Angels light the way, so that all darkness vanishes and you are standing in a light so bright and clear that you can understand all things you see.'

A COURSE IN MIRACLES

Archangels are a powerful choir of angels who are dedicated to health and healing on a planetary level. These phenomenal beings are helping people all over the world make the transition to peace. They are an interesting 'force' of angels – the ultimate peaceful warriors – and when they arrive you can't help but feel their presence.

As we already know, archangels are the 'managers' of our guardian angels. They are the next step up and they mean business. I've seen many images of archangels that are soft, fluffy and gentle, but I have to say these beings are strong, warrior-like and powerful. They have a role to fulfil and nothing is going to stop them. Saying that, of course these beings are ultimately full of the love of God. They don't judge in any way, but when we open up to their help they will be swift, direct and to the point. I truly believe archangels are the beings we need on our side. They'll work with our guardian angels to support us if we're open to their help.

There are probably thousands of archangels out there in the universe, but some are better known to us than others and we'll look at four of the main ones later in this chapter.

We know now that angels are actually formless beings, pure divine energy, but they show themselves to us in a human or even superhuman form so we can understand them as beings and also the magnitude of their power. Archangels are no different. For that reason you'll see many different descriptions of archangels and interpretations of their energy, but their essence is without doubt exactly the same.

Archangels as guardian angels?

I've heard of many cases where people have had interaction with a specific archangel or have mentioned to me that when they asked their guardian angel to reveal themselves, they heard the name of an archangel. These people probably have experienced this archangel in their meditation practice or have connected with them in another way. But it's important to say that the major archangels can't be our own personal guardian angels. These beings aren't exclusive to any one person but open to us all. So, when it comes to hearing an archangel's name as that of your guardian angel, it is likely that what's happening is your guardian angel has the same name as one of the major archangels. 'Uriel', 'Gabriel' and even 'Michael' are probably just like the common names 'John', 'Mary', etc., down here on Earth.

Our guardian angels are with us all of the time, but archangels have to be invited to join us. We can do this anytime.

One important thing to know is that archangels are multi-dimensional beings. This means they can be in many places at once. In fact neither angels or archangels are limited by time or space – their energy is eternal and everywhere.

Archangels

The best-known archangels have major roles in helping this planet. Here is some more detailed information about Michael, Gabriel, Raphael and Uriel.

Archangel Michael: The protector

Archangel Michael is the king of the angels, the prince of heaven and the patron saint of protection. Old Catholic imagery shows him slaying the devil or forcing him into purgatory. I have found this to be a metaphor for helping us overcome the darkness of our ego. Archangel Michael protects us from that challenging and sometimes dark voice in our mind that holds us back and makes us feel we aren't good enough.

When I see Michael, I see him as a tall muscular man with blond locks. He wears armour and carries a sword. The sword is made of fiery light and is a sword of truth. It can light up the darkness surrounding a situation and also remove the illusions, fears or challenges that are holding us back. When Michael's sword of light touches anything that is fearful rather than loving, it turns it into light, so it dispels any darkness.

Michael can be called upon by anyone at any time. He has a bright blue energy and we can invoke his presence by visualizing ourselves cloaked in a blue light. His purpose is to protect and guide all who call on him.

Michael's legions

Archangel Michael has an army of angels. These divine beings are dedicated to the protection of humanity. As you know, angels can't help us unless we welcome them in, but these beings will do their best to guard, guide and protect those who are desperate. They are often found in areas where wars and fear-driven violence are taking place. They are peaceful warriors dedicated to the wellbeing of all humanity.

Lightworkers

Archangel Michael has something of a soft spot for the lightworkers of this planet. A lightworker is someone who has been called to help others, a person who dedicates themselves to others and their spiritual growth, whether they realize it or not. Most lightworkers generally aren't aware of their special gifts or talents because they're the most modest, selfless people you'll ever meet. But when a lightworker follows their divine path to help others, Michael's energy and legions join them and support their journey to service.

Cutting the cords

One of the great gifts that Archangel Michael offers to us is the removal of the cords. I've written about this elsewhere, but it's worth reiterating here, as it's one of the greatest spiritual practices I've ever experienced. The cords are the connections that bind us to people, places or memories that are filled with fear. When we're exposed to a situation that's challenging or emotional, or someone with a draining personality comes into contact with us, a cord can hook onto us and bind us to that energy. The energy may not be harmful *per se*, but it can become a barrier to the peace, happiness and balance that we deserve.

Some cords are more challenging than others. For example, I've worked with mental health support workers with challenging patients who demand a lot of them. I'll never forget one woman. She loved her work and was dedicated to it, but when she came home it was as if her mind couldn't switch off from worrying about her patients. I remember asking her if she'd ever considered spiritual protection and saying some 'disconnecting prayers' in the evenings. She'd never even thought of it. I offered her a daily protection visualization and a prayer to cut the cords in the evening. I spoke to her about it some weeks later and she said she was sleeping better than ever and that it was as if a weight had been lifted from her shoulders. In a spiritual sense, it had been.

See page 160 for techniques on cord-cutting and protection.

A prayer to invoke Michael

Dear Archangel Michael,

Thank you for your protective light and presence in my life.

It feels so positive and reassuring to know that you and your angels are keeping me safe on all levels.

I welcome your sword of truth and light cutting anything from my life and path that's not serving me so I can make room for the goodness I deserve.

I am safe in your presence.

Thank you, Michael!

And so it is!

Archangel Gabriel: The nurturer

Gabriel is one of the most loving and nurturing angels I've ever experienced. Most people expect this angel to be male, but I've always seen Gabriel as a strong, curvaceous female with flowing red locks and bright turquoise eyes. She has the appearance of a maternal angel, but a fiery one at that. I have often compared her look to that of the beautiful singer Adele and I was pleasantly surprised to hear a while back that Adele called her son Angelo – could this be a sign? When you hear Adele you know she is someone who has joy in her core. She loves laughter, but honesty is everything with her. She just can't lie. These are qualities that Gabriel has too. Fascinating.

'Gabriel' means 'strength of God' and the purpose of this angel is to nurture and guide the children of God. We are all the children of God, of course, and we all have an inner child within us too. Most of us have forgotten about this child, but when we stop acknowledging this very divine aspect of ourselves we can shut off our feelings completely. One of the greatest gifts Gabriel offers us is the opportunity to send this inner child love and nurturing through our prayers and visualizations.

Fertility and pregnancy

In the Bible Gabriel is said to be the angel who came to Mary to tell her of the coming birth of her son Jesus. Gabriel also appeared to Zacharias to tell him about the birth of his son, John the Baptist. Since these early stories, Gabriel has been known as the angel of children and fertility.

Gabriel can help those who are trying to conceive a child and can help through all aspects of pregnancy, including labour. She has the amazing ability to put both mother and child at ease.

Communication

Gabriel is not only the angel of mothers but also the angel of communication. She carries the trumpet of good news and all through written history there have been accounts of her arriving with good news or passing on some sort of knowledge.

Linked to this is one of the greatest services this divine angel offers: helping us to speak our truth. There are so many people in the world who are walking around with extra baggage on their chest: the feeling that they can't share their true emotions. Gabriel can help us let go of this baggage. She can help us speak with truth and integrity in our heart and she can help us feel safe when we do this.

When we offer someone our heartfelt truth, we are giving them a gift. Even if the information is challenging or deeply emotional, when we release it we open ourselves to new positive experiences. On a spiritual level, when we're holding something in or not sharing how we truly feel, we're coming from a space in our heart that is fear-based. When we do this, we're creating barriers and blocks to receiving the abundance of love that is all around us. This is why Gabriel helps us to speak our truth.

Leaders and speakers

As Gabriel carries the trumpet of good news and is the angel of communication, she can be called upon by leaders, speakers and even teachers for help in getting their message out loud and clear.

Gabriel will help you speak from the heart too, without a doubt, but it's important to point out that if you ask for her help, there won't be any lies coming from your mouth – she will urge you in some way to tell *all* of the truth and nothing else.

A prayer to invoke Gabriel

Dear Gabriel, archangel of pure nurturing love,

Thank you for shining your energy over my life.

I allow you to work with me in sharing my truths with integrity and for the highest good of my spiritual growth.

Thank you, too, for helping me see through the eyes of my inner child so I can see that life is full of opportunity, joy and wonder.

It feels so good to know your maternal guiding light is in my heart today.

And so it is!

Archangel Raphael: The healer

Raphael's name means 'God heals' and he is the angel of healing. He is a beautiful angel and I'll never forget the first time I experienced his healing presence. I saw him wash over a person and their energy with healing and it was such a beautiful sight that every hair on my body stood on end. I was overcome with emotion and couldn't contain the love I felt. I began to cry...

Raphael can bring healing miracles to anyone who really allows them to happen and his bright emerald light can help us on all levels – mental, emotional, physical and spiritual.

When I see Raphael in my meditations and through clairvoyance I see him as a young, handsome Italian-looking man. He has a strong jawline and beautiful golden eyes. He has curly hair and his smile is so welcoming. His aura is bright emerald with rainbows and the lightest of violet swirls.

In artwork Raphael is seen carrying the caduceus, which is the universal symbol of healing that you will often see on the side of ambulances. This always reminds me that Raphael's healing light is available to all those who welcome it.

Healing and health professionals

As Raphael is the angel of healing, he acts as a spiritual guide to all medical, health and healing professionals who live their life in service to the wellbeing of others. If you are a health professional yourself, or have a close friend who is, and there are challenges along your path, you can invite Raphael to support you. He'll work with your guardian angel to prompt you in the right direction.

Raphael loves energy healers, therapists and practitioners. If you are one yourself and invite him in, he can guide your whole practice. You can welcome him in to light up the room with healing light and of course to help you heal others. He is ready and willing to help you with everything from Reiki and crystal therapy to chakra work. Call on him to be present whenever you're focusing on your healing work.

Healing in the now

Raphael can also be called upon to bring healing to you personally. One of the greatest messages he brings to us is that healing occurs in the present moment. Generally, people pray for healing and hope that the future will deliver the answer, or ask for healing of something that was diagnosed in the past. When we acknowledge something of the past or ask about the future, we're letting our present be influenced by these thoughts. But when we welcome Raphael's healing, we can do it in such a way that we know it's happening this second. Right now, this very minute and hour, is when miracles happen.

Protection while travelling

Raphael is also the angel to call on while travelling. One of the greatest gifts he offers us is being able to feel as comfortable and well as possible when on the move. Even if we're a good traveller, he can help us relax and be well. If we suffer from travel sickness or are feeling uptight about a journey, we can speak to him and he'll be there with us, supporting us every step of the way.

I travel often, generally by air, and I always invite Raphael to be with me. One of the things that seems to happen to me is that I fall asleep as soon as I get on the flight – even before take-off! Then I wake up and I'm either landing or I'm 10 minutes away from landing. It's miraculous. Thank you, Raphael!

A prayer to invoke Raphael

Archangel Raphael, divine healer,

Thank you for surrounding me in your emerald healing rays so that I can accept the wellbeing I deserve.

I allow healing to take place on all levels in my body, mind and soul at this very moment.

Thank you for leading the way on all of my journeys.

Whether they are internal or external, I know you will keep me well.

And so it is!

Archangel Uriel: The lightbringer

Archangel Uriel is the angel I relate to most. He's bright and full of life and energy. His name means 'God's light' and he reminds me of a bright summer's day. His purpose is to bring in the light of God.

One of the great things I've found about Uriel is that he can really cheer you up. Because he holds the true qualities of light, he brings with him everything that a holiday on the beach would. Joy, happiness and rejuvenation radiate from his aura, and he wants to make us feel good and positive while we're here on planet Earth.

When I've seen Uriel in my meditations he's always appeared as a handsome young-looking angel. He has blond hair but is sunkissed. He has little sun freckles on his cheeks and wears a muscle-sculpted top of armour made out of a type of metal that I've never seen on this planet. He carries a torch of light, which represents his ability to remove darkness and bring a situation back into balance.

As Uriel is the angel of light, he can help with any dark thoughts or illusions. If you're feeling confused about the answer to an issue or searching for the solution to something in your life, he'll help you tap into your intuition to figure it out.

The solar plexus

The solar plexus energy centre is found just above the navel. This is your power centre – the sun centre of your body. If the energy around this part of your body is unbalanced or blocked, there is a good chance you'll be experiencing a lot of frustration and built-up anger and will lack energy. Uriel's light comes directly into this space and busts through the blocks that are stopping you from being energetically driven the way that you deserve to be, so you can be motivated, insightful and focused in all that you do.

Tests and exams

Uriel is a brilliant angel to call on for help when you're going through a test or exam. He helps your head feel carefree and alert so you can access your memories and experiences loud and clear.

Shining your light

If you've special gifts and talents to share, then Archangel Uriel is your new best friend. He can help you have the confidence and self-belief to share your uniqueness with the world.

One of the main messages that came through when I began to work with this amazing angel was that he looks at us all and sees our creative potential. He wants us all to have a place in the world and doesn't see anyone as 'more special' than anyone else. He simply sees us all for who we are.

If you feel you have a special talent or gift to share with this planet and have been holding back for too long, invoke Uriel's presence and allow his light to dispel your doubts so you can really express who you are.

Self-employed individuals

Uriel loves to help those who are self-employed. He knows more than any other angel how challenging it can be to put your services out there and how easy it is for your vision to be clouded by your ego and fears. He comes to you like a bright ray of light and shines light on your business so you can attract all those to whom you can be of service for the highest good.

If you know of anyone who's struggling with their business or you have challenges in yours, call on Uriel. He'll come in with ideas and inspiration and help you seek a solution to any challenges you face.

A prayer to invoke Uriel

Archangel Uriel, bringer of light,

Thank you for inspiring me so I can share my gifts, talents and self with the world.

I allow your light to shine over me as I connect with my inner voice and power source to feel inspired and creative.

I am bathed in the light of God.

Thank you for showing it to me!

And so it is!

An affirmation to invoke Uriel

I shine my light with the world and embrace my gifts as I'm guided by Archangel Uriel!

Exercise: Sending help from the archangels

In this exercise we are going to work with Archangel Raphael and Archangel Michael and his legion of angels. This world requires so much healing, protection and freedom and these angels are without doubt dedicated to one thing: love.

Whenever love is present, there is healing, there is safety and there is freedom, and this is truly what many people and places need today. As good people of this planet, we can help bring this about with our thoughts and prayers. Prayers really do have the power to move people and change their lives, and I know for a fact that when we send angels to other people, they hear our call and will do their best to offer support.

Let us now take some time to think about places that are in desperate need and send our thoughts, angels and prayers to them.

❖ Take some time to yourself. It's better if you're not disturbed, not because it'll stop the healing or prayers, but because that way you can focus more easily.

❖ Sit quietly and comfortably and focus on your breath. You can keep your eyes open or close them if that feels better to you.

❖ Think about places, people and situations in the world, or in your own life, that could benefit from the light of angels.

❖ In your mind, imagine a host of angels led by two powerful archangels descending on this space. See in your mind and feel in your heart their light shining all over this space. See golden light shining through every crack, every space, every person there, and lighting up every face and heart.

❖ See the host of angels swirling, dancing, healing and loving this situation and all involved. Imagine peace filling up all the available space and washing away anything that isn't love.

❖ Then say the following prayer:

By the Grace of God,

Thank you, dear angels, Archangel Michael and Archangel Raphael, for lighting up the people, places and situations that I feel need your love.

Thank you for leading them to peace, thank you for leading them to love and thank you for sending your healing angels to lead them to harmony.

I surrender my worries about this to you, as I know you will do your best to heal, protect, guide and guard, all for the highest good.

And so it is!

❖ Take some moments to allow your intentions to be set. Quietly thank your Creator and the angels for helping you set your healing thoughts.

❖ If you're able to do so, you may want to light a white candle at the window to support your prayer and focus on peace.

SUMMARY 🖎

❖ Archangels are the 'boss angels' who ensure all the other angels are performing their duties properly.

❖ They are warrior angels filled with love and peace.

❖ Archangel Michael is the ultimate angel of protection.

❖ Archangel Gabriel can help us connect with our inner child.

❖ Archangel Raphael is the angel of healing.

❖ Archangel Uriel lights up the darkness and helps us find solutions to challenges.

Chapter 8
Healing angels

*'Millions of spiritual creatures walk
the earth unseen, both when we
wake and when we sleep.'*

JOHN MILTON

Healing angels are a choir of angels that are dedicated
to healing the world. They are mesmerizing. I've seen
them many times and they have the purest light I've ever
seen. Their auras shine brightly and they have golden,
white and often emerald hues all around them.

Healing angels serve humanity. They are here to help us
overcome the health challenges that we can face while
on Earth. They pour their light into the sick and guide
many back to health.

These divine physicians are led by no other than
Archangel Raphael. Whenever you ask them for healing,
they'll place their hands upon you and wish you well.

Faith

I've always been fascinated by faith. They say it can move mountains and I believe this to be so. Faith is dedication, it is remembering, it is deconditioning the mind from fear and directing it to the source of our creation. When we have faith in angels, they do deliver. The reason for this is we let go of our fears of being let down and disappointed, we hand our situation over to them and we trust that they will resolve it.

Ever since I was young I've loved the idea of saying a prayer for another person. When I was growing up, a close family friend called Margaret often looked after me while my parents were working. She was a devout Catholic and if it was the weekend she would sometimes take me along with her to church. I remember one night standing by her side as she lit candles and kneeled down with her hands in the prayer position. I asked her what she was doing and she told me she was praying for her family. The power, the love and the hope that were in her at that moment have stayed with me ever since. And since discovering angels, I've constantly said prayers for others in the hope that angels will guide them on their path.

I've realized that no matter what your faith is, it helps. As I've said, angels go beyond religion, but if you've a specific belief system they'll support you in following it to the best of your ability as long as it's for your growth and for the highest good of all.

An encounter with the healing angels

Earlier this year I had a wonderful encounter with the healing angels. I was in my office in Glasgow preparing for the day ahead when a golden and emerald light filled up the room. Clairvoyantly I could sense there were angels present and I hadn't even tuned myself in to work. I knew something was happening.

I closed my eyes and in my mind I could see a tall slim male angel standing there. All around him was a shimmering golden light. In my mind I asked why he was present at this time and I was told, 'All will soon be revealed. I am a healing angel!'

His message was direct and simple, and the most important thing was that I trusted it. I had an urge to go the door and open it. I wasn't due to begin work for another 35 minutes, but something almost *made* me do it!

Standing behind the door was a sweet-looking woman. She was in her sixties, wore glasses and had blow-dried hair. She was all wrapped up in winter clothes, with matching scarf and gloves. Looking at me, she said, 'Sorry I'm a little bit early.'

As I looked back at her and smiled, I saw the angel from my vision standing behind her. Instantly I opened the door wide and welcomed her in.

She sat down and I offered her a glass of water. (I keep a cooler in my office.) She accepted and admitted she was quite parched.

'I don't know if you'll be able to help me,' she said, shaking my hand. 'My name is Emily.'

I realized then that this lady had booked a reading, but I felt as if more was going to happen. Not only was it as if the divine had perfectly orchestrated her being early and me being organized so that we could connect, but I knew that the angels had encouraged her to come and see me, not because I could 'fix' her but because I could create the right space so that she could fix herself, with their help. I knew at that moment that something miraculous was going to take place in front of me.

I told Emily how I worked and invited her to place her hands on top of my angel cards. Then I closed my eyes and placed my hands on top of hers. There in my mind stood the angel.

'We've brought Emily to you so that we can help her overcome the challenges she is going through,' he said. 'All through her life Emily has acted like an Earth angel, giving, delivering and placing herself in complete service to others. Many years ago we sent urges for her to slow down, but she never trusted them and continued to serve. Now, years on, she is tired and cancer has spread around her body. We want her to live, as many rely on her and we want to help heal her. Can you tell her we are here?'

Every hair on my body was standing on end. I felt overwhelmed and emotional, but I knew I had to hold it together to bring this message to Emily. I told her what I'd heard and she responded emotionally.

'I have been fighting this cancer,' she told me. 'I've had so many different treatments and I'm not sure how much more I can take. I tell everyone I'm fine, but I'm not. I'm scared. I believe in God, but I think I'm dying.'

I told Emily that I believed differently. Angels had sent her to me. They wanted her to know that they were here to heal her. She just needed to get on their wavelength for it to happen.

'Emily must know,' the healing angel told me, 'that she can only heal if she stops fighting her cancer. When she is "fighting", it is creating a war in her body. We are here to replace this with harmony.'

At that moment it was if I had a download from heaven. The angel had brought something to my awareness that it was important to share: when we have a challenge in our body, we often want to fight it. When we fight, though, even with our mental power, we're creating a war inside our body. And the true healer of dis-ease is not war but *love*. You see, dis-ease is fear, it's not real, and even though we experience it in our body, it isn't who we are. We are *love* and when we remember this and focus on it, we become whole again.

Emily was at the stage of giving up and the angels didn't want that to happen. They wanted her to stay and continue her journey with her family. To do that, she just needed to change the way she thought and felt about her body.

The healing angels encouraged me to facilitate a space where Emily could invoke them and ultimately heal herself by opening up to their light. So I invited her to lie on the Reiki bed in my office and told her that she needed to welcome the angels in and that I'd help her do it. We had enough time for her to lie down, relax and allow the healing to unfold. As she lay down, the angels told me to say, 'Lymphoma,' and she told me that that was the first form the cancer had taken.

I opened my mouth and began to speak. 'Emily, you are already whole, you are already healed. The energy in your body is flowing, free and harmonious.'

Sitting at her feet, I placed my hands on either side of her legs and prayed out loud: 'Thank you, angels, healing angels, Archangel Raphael and anyone else who can help. Thank you for pouring your healing light into Emily so that she can truly perceive that she is already whole and complete. We surrender this moment to you and allow you to do your work for the highest good! And so it is!'

Emily's eyes were closed, but I could see teardrops rolling down her face. She was finally surrendering – she was giving up the war, she was letting dis-ease out and she was letting healing in.

Angels surrounded the bed that day – it was lit up with golden energy. It was a pleasure to experience it. I knew in my heart and soul that Emily was going to be fine and that she was going to live for many happy and healthy years to come.

After the session we hugged and she went on her way. I later received messages from her to say that the doctors had agreed her cancer was going into remission – but she already knew that! God bless her!

We are already whole

The message of the healing angels is that we are already whole. They are here to remind us of this. Our true self, our soul, can't be harmed or tainted. It is always healed, because it is unconditional love. Our body, on the other hand, can go through challenges and face dis-ease if we don't know about the wholeness of who we are.

When we call upon the healing angels, they encourage us to have faith and remember who we are. They send their healing rays to remove the blocks in our perception that stand between us and wholeness. We ultimately heal ourselves, but we are supported by these divine beings as we do so.

Healing ourselves

We don't need to see angels to ask them for healing. We can call on them at any time to bless us with their light. If you're experiencing a challenge in your body and have been fighting it, now is your opportunity to change. Changing the way you feel about your body helps you break down the barriers of fear that are stopping healing taking place. If, for example, there's a specific ailment you're experiencing or a particular organ connected to your dis-ease, it would be interesting to see how you think about it. Ask yourself honestly about it and see it in your inner vision. If you feel frustration or anger or even hate for it, this is blocking healing.

Angels have taught me that when people fall ill, they often become frustrated by their body and ask, 'Why is this happening to me?' or, even worse, 'Why is my body doing this to me?' These are cries for help for sure, but they're also clear indicators that these people have forgotten that they are already whole.

Most of us will allow our body to decide how we are feeling. But the healing angels brought this message through that I would love to share with you:

> 'Your body does not decide how your health is, your mind does. How you feel, think, act and react from your mind and heart affects your body. If your intentions, acts and thoughts are aligned with love, then sure enough, your body will be too. If your mind and intentions are filled with resentment, grievances or grudges, then these emotions will be turned into something physical within. If fear-based ideas are changed to love-based truths, physical, emotional and mental healing can take place from the inside out. We are here to help you do this. We invite you to remember the love you are and allow the healing to unfold from there.'

Changing your thoughts and ideas may take some time, especially if they've been present for a while. No worries, though – angels can help you do that too.

Many of us need to heal our thoughts and this is one of the purposes of the divine healing angels who are just waiting to help us.

> **A prayer to align your thoughts with healing and love**
>
> *Thank you, divine healing angels, for supporting me as I release the thoughts that are no longer serving me so I can align with my soul's truth, which is whole, complete and healed. I align myself with love.*
>
> *And so it is!*

Prayers of grace

As I mentioned earlier, I love the idea of praying for others. In fact it is something I do often. When we pray for those who need support with their health, healing angels go to them. Just take a moment to think about the fact that every time you've thought about someone in need, no matter who they are or where they are, and have asked God to help them, a divine healing angel has gone to them and blessed them with their presence, even if it has remained unseen.

When you pray for another person you're giving them the gift of grace and opening up opportunities for miracles to happen for them. Many people write and e-mail me for prayers or ask me to pray for them. I always do!

I've learned, however, that when we pray for others it's important to do it for their highest good. For example, if someone asks me to pray for their mother's health and their mother is near the end of her journey on Earth, sure I'll send healing prayers and angels, but that might not mean she's going to recover. Instead the healing angels may support her and comfort her so that she can be safe and protected as she makes the natural transition to heaven.

Another thing is, what if the person you are praying for doesn't want the help? Or what if they do but are unable to ask for it themselves? Will it still be available? This is where grace steps in.

What this means is that if a person is unable to ask for help, for whatever reason, even though their soul desperately requires it, the Law of Grace can overcome their 'free will' so that they can accept the healing they deserve. And if they don't want to accept the help we are praying for, we won't be on the receiving end of any karma. Perfect!

To ensure this happens, just add 'under the Law of Grace' or 'according to the Law of Grace' to your prayers.

Healing hands

Do you remember falling over as a child? Do you remember bumping your leg and a loving parent covering the bump with their hand and reminding you that you were OK? That was your first contact with hands-on healing.

We all have the ability to heal others with our hands, and angels can help us. Giving someone one of these 'angel healing experiences' is a brilliant way to develop your connection and trust with the angelic realm. This was one of the first ways I developed my ability to be in tune with the angels.

By placing your hands on the shoulders of a friend or loved one you can call on the angels to send their healing rays through you and your hands into the other person. In this instance you become the channel, the Earth angel who passes on this very natural healing to your 'client'.

In my angel workshops I often encourage people to partner up to give and to receive an angel healing for 10 minutes just to experience what it's like. I recently did it with an audience of over 100 people in London and I was overwhelmed by the feedback. Both 'healer' and 'client' experienced feelings of love and other positive sensations throughout the healing process.

According to *A Course in Miracles*, 'It is as blessed to give as to receive,' and that's entirely true. When we offer someone healing, we receive it too. As we welcome the healing in and allow it to pass through our body in order to pass it on, we receive it ourselves, and then, as we send it, the universe blesses us with the same light tenfold!

When I left school I went to work in a hairdressing salon. I was only 15 when I started. I'd wash people's hair, clean up and make tea and coffee, plus my boss showed me how to give people a shoulder massage while they were waiting for the stylist to cut their hair. This was the perfect opportunity to offer angel healing.

After being in the job a few weeks I managed to pluck up the courage to begin offering angel healing to the clients. I'd give them a massage and then for the final five minutes I'd lightly place my hands on their shoulders and invite the angels to send their healing rays to them through me. I was amazed at the feedback I received, but not only that, I saw things too.

I'll never forget the time I gave angel healing to a woman who was always a pleasure to talk to. I explained to her my interest in angels and healing and said I could share some with her, then I invited her to close her eyes and said I would lightly hold her shoulders and pass on the good intentions. As I did this, I could feel my body heating up and see purples and indigo blue swirls in my mind.

Standing there with my eyes closed, holding her shoulders, I allowed the healing to unfold. After the five minutes or so, I encouraged her to come back and open her eyes. She said, 'Wow, that was amazing. Thank you!'

I knew she meant more but probably didn't want to sound mad, so I said, 'I could see blues and purples swirling in my mind when I was doing it.'

'No way, no way! You're freaking me out!' she said.

I began to laugh.

'I saw that too,' she continued, 'and thought you'd think I was going off my head if I told you!'

Angels often show themselves to us when we are sending or receiving healing and I believe that this lovely lady's angels had auras of blue and purple.

If you open yourself up to offering healing to loved ones, there's a great chance you'll develop your abilities to see, hear or even feel your guardian angels and the angels of those you are healing as you do so. It's very easy to try. See the exercise on page 101.

Reiki and spiritual healing

There are many different systems of energy healing out there in the world now and Reiki and spiritual healing are amongst the most popular. Healing angels work with Reiki practitioners and spiritual healers, whether they realize it or not! These angels stand by, protect, guide and support, and often allow the therapist to intuit which part of their client's body needs healing the most.

If you're a practitioner of an energy healing system, you might like to acknowledge the healing angels before you begin any treatments. I've practised Reiki for over 10 years now and I always welcome the healing and Reiki angels into my practice. I always like to know I've asked for as much help as possible!

Sending healing thoughts and prayers

If you want to send healing to someone you can't see at a particular time or you just know someone needs extra support, you can do this in their absence. Healing angels aren't limited by time and space and can deliver your healing intentions at any time.

So, how do you do it?

Visualize healing angels

You can visualize the person you feel needs healing surrounded by angels. I like to visualize them surrounded by angels who are placing their healing hands on them. As the angels' hands touch the person, they transfer golden light into them. It's a beautiful thought.

You can do anything you want with your visualization. Even just cocooning your friend or loved one in pink light will allow the healing angels to go to them. Just remember to have the intention in place 'all for the highest good' and 'under the Law of Grace' so that their soul can accept the healing for them!

A Prayer of healing for those in need

Archangel Raphael and divine healing angels,

Thank you for blessing [name of person] with your healing rays and presence. It is so good to see them returning to their natural state of good health and to see the peace of this in their eyes.

I surrender this to you under the Law of Grace and so it is!

Exercise: Sharing angel healing

Now we've come to the point where we can learn how to offer angel healing to a loved one. The most important thing is to do it with the best of intentions and of course with their permission.

Healing is completely natural. It's encouraging someone to return to love and when you offer it to someone you're just hosting the space for them to receive it. Even though there may not be a major illness or dis-ease present, healing will bring harmony and peace to both giver and receiver.

❖ Ensure you will not be disturbed for a while.

❖ It is best to have your 'client' sitting in a chair.

❖ Ask them to close their eyes and place your hands lightly on their shoulders.

❖ Closing your eyes, begin to imagine a healing light coming into your body from above your head and exiting through your hands.

❖ As the energy comes from your hands, allow it to wash into the whole of your client's being.

❖ As that happens, you can say a prayer, either silently to yourself or out loud if you feel comfortable doing it that way. I suggest something along the lines of:

> *Divine healing angels,*
>
> *Thank you for pouring your healing light into [client's .name]. I offer you my hands to use as your healing instrument. Thank you for passing all your positive vibrations into this very deserving person.*
>
> *And so it is!*

✦   Then allow the healing to flow. It may only last for a few minutes or you may feel yourself holding on for 10–15 minutes. Just keep doing it for as long as you feel is right and at the end just say internally, 'Thank you, angels!' to acknowledge their gift to you.

SUMMARY 🖎

✦   Angels work with our faith to heal us.

✦   Knowing we are already whole allows healing to occur.

✦   Hands-on healing is natural – we all can do it.

✦   We can send healing angels to others with grace.

✦   Reiki, spiritual healing and other energy healing practices are guided by angels.

Chapter 9
Seeing angels

'Faith causes the unseen to become visible.'
ERNEST HOLMES, SPIRITUAL WRITER AND TEACHER

People say being able to see angels is a gift and it really is! But what I've found is that it's not offered to just a few people. We can all do it – with practice. At some point on our life's journey we'll all have experienced clairvoyance. Clairvoyance means 'clear seeing'. It's the psychic ability to see things beyond the everyday world. The most common form is having some sort of experience through dreams. When you've had a dream in which you've seen a future event or been visited by a loved one in heaven or by angels, that's clairvoyance.

All clairvoyants see things differently and the reason for this is that we all see things differently in life. If you and I were standing at the top of a mountain together and were looking out over the view, I guarantee that each of us would pick out different objects, clouds and even landmarks.

You've probably realized by now that angels adapt themselves to us so we can understand them to the best of our ability, and it's the same with clairvoyance: angels will work with us in a way that is understandable and accessible to us.

The way I see angels has fluctuated over the years. It generally happens in my mind. I'll be looking at someone, or a space, and in my mind, at the same time as seeing the person or space, I'll see an angel there. It's as if my mind is projecting the image it's seeing into that space so that I can see and understand what's going on angelically.

At first when I saw angels it would happen almost by chance – I'd just be in the right place at the right time. When I wanted to see one, it didn't always happen. I had to learn how to develop my sight.

Developing the sight

When I started developing my clairvoyance I'd practise doing readings for people and in my mind I'd say, 'Angels, please show yourselves to me.' Sometimes my prayer would be answered, but most of the time it wouldn't be. Things were different, though, if I closed my eyes but still faced the person I was reading for. Then I'd see a light, a colour, an outline or, even better, an angel standing there.

I believe we have all seen our angels. Before we came to Earth our soul was connected to our angel. The problem is that even though that connection is still present, we feel separate from our angel because we can't see it. I've found that remembering, believing and even simply trusting that we are one with these divine beings allows us to see them once more.

Baby steps

Taking baby steps is the best way forwards. This is because many people love the idea of seeing angels but at the back of their mind they have reservations or even find it scary. When I started to develop my clairvoyance I had these reservations too, but ultimately it became the most exciting, purpose-filled part of my life.

The aura and chakras

A great place to start developing clairvoyance is by looking at the aura. You'll remember that this is the psychic energy that surrounds every living thing. It is almost like a mirror, a mirror of the soul. It contains information about a person's life – past, present and what they are focusing on now that will create their future. The best thing about the aura is the fact that it's connected to the angels. Our guardian angel is so close to us that they're actually standing in our aura, and once we start to see our aura, eventually their aura will become apparent too. Exciting, right?

Before we begin practising seeing angels and auras, though, it's important to address the psychic sight. We 'see' psychically by a process of 'tuning in' our energy. The way I do it is by visualizing the specific energy centres in my body that allow me to perceive heaven. You may have heard of these centres before. They are called the chakras.

Chakras

Chakra is a Sanskrit word that means 'wheel' and it is used to describe a spiritual energy point on the body. There are seven main chakras running from the base of the spine to the top of the head. Each one has both physical and non-physical connections.

✦ The first chakra is found at the base of the spine. It is known as Muladhara, which means 'root support'. This chakra is red and is connected to our foundations, such as our home, family, finances and comfort zone.

✦ The second chakra is found just below the navel and is known as Svadisthana, which means 'one's own place'. This centre, the sacral chakra, is orange and is connected to our reproductive system and sexual organs.

✦ The third chakra is found at our stomach and is known as Manipura, which means 'place of jewels'. This chakra is yellow and is connected to our willpower, drive and energy.

✦ The fourth chakra is found in our heart centre and is known as Anahata, which means 'unstruck'. This chakra is green and is connected to our ability to give and receive love.

✦ The fifth chakra is found at the throat area and is known as Vishuddha, which means 'pure place'. This chakra is blue and is connected to our communication and ability to speak with integrity.

✦ The sixth chakra is found between the brows and is known as Ajna, which means 'command'. This chakra, the third eye, is indigo. It is connected to our mind and perception, and governs our ability to see clairvoyantly.

✦ The seventh chakra is found at the top of the head and is known as Sahasrara, which means 'lotus of 1,000 petals'. This chakra, the crown, is violet. It is connected to our spiritual connections and beliefs.

Exercise: Activating your psychic sight

Your psychic sight is governed by the sixth chakra, known as Ajna or the third eye centre. When you want to activate your clairvoyance, you must open up this chakra like a door. Through that door you'll see heaven and the spiritual worlds.

✦ Opening up your third eye centre is simple. All you have to do is close your eyes and imagine yourself surrounded by a golden light of protection.

✦ In your mind, visualize your guardian angel standing behind you. See them standing with their wings around you so that you're safe and protected.

✦ When you've done this, visualize an eye between your brows. This eye is larger than normal and is closed.

✦ With the power of your mind, see it open up.

✦ With your own eyes still closed, take note of your third eye – its colour, how it looks.

❖   When your third eye is open, you can also open up your other eyes. Notice how you see the world around you – it may be slightly different.

Once you've tried out some of the following psychic exercises, it is super-important to close your third eye (see *page 114*).

Exercise: Aura gazing

Aura gazing, perhaps unsurprisingly, involves gazing at someone's aura. You can practise with a partner, or even a pet, just to get an idea of their energy.

❖   Have the partner (or pet) sit on a chair in front of, ideally, a white or neutral background and close your eyes.

❖   Centre yourself. Imagine your own light around you and your guardian angel behind you.

❖   Once you feel relaxed and focused on your breath, open your eyes and look towards your partner. Allow yourself to gaze at them without blinking. Almost stare at them. I always look at their third eye centre to begin with and allow myself to move into a light trance.

❖   As you gaze at them, you may see a light projecting from their body or even see a colour around them.

❖   Do this for a few moments then share your experiences and write them down in your journal for future reference.

An alternative

If you find seeing the aura quite difficult this way, there is another way. What I do if I can't see the aura is to ask something like 'If this person's aura were a specific colour, what colour would it be?' and then I see a flash of that colour in my mind. Trust the first colour that comes to you.

Exercise: Angel gazing

You can use the aura-gazing technique for 'angel gazing'. For example, say you're practising on your friend, you can follow exactly the same procedure except that this time you hold the intention of seeing their guardian angel rather than seeing their aura.

It's all down to *intention*, so trust everything that you see or that comes through for you.

Your imagination

Your imagination is your friend when it comes to developing your psychic senses. Just keep asking yourself questions like 'If there were an angel standing behind me right now, what would it look like?' or making statements like 'If there were an angel with my friend [name] right now, it would look like...' or even 'If my pet's aura were a colour right now, it would be...' and allow your imagination to paint a picture in your mind. That's how you develop your psychic sight!

Colour information

When you begin to gaze at auras or see the auras of angels you'll be able to start building up information that will be relevant for you and whoever you're working with. Here's some information about the colours you'll see and what they can represent:

Red
Aura: Foundations, strength, courage, financial support, safety.

Angel message: Your guardian angel is bringing strength to support you in all areas of your life, particularly with security and material needs.

Pink
Aura: Love, nurturing, mothering, peace.

Angel message: Your angel wants you to know that you are loved unconditionally and that if you realize this you will break the barriers that are holding you back in life.

Orange
Aura: Excitement, creativity, movement, going with the flow.

Angel message: Your guardian angel is bringing harmony and peace to your world so you can go with the flow.

Yellow
Aura: Joy, happiness, energy, willpower.

Angel message: Your guardian angel is encouraging you to do what makes you happy. This will help you feel strong and powerful again.

Green
Aura: Generosity, healing, emotions, forgiveness.

Angel message: Your guardian angel is bringing you healing and support to help you feel well and balanced.

Blue
Aura: Communication, openness, truth, independence, freedom, emotions.

Angel message: Your guardian angel wants you to know that you're not on your own and it's OK to be emotional.

Turquoise
Aura: Teaching, learning, nature.

Angel message: Your guardian angel wants you to see every challenging experience as a learning experience.

Indigo
Aura: Psychic abilities, dreaming, logic, mindfulness.

Angel message: Your guardian angel is sending you messages through dreams, signs and visions. Keep an open mind and trust your instincts.

Violet

Aura: Spirituality, awareness, God, intelligence, a strong mind.

Angel message: Your guardian angel wants you to know you are an old soul. You are never separate from God and you are cleverer than you give yourself credit for.

Magenta

Aura: Divine timing, patience, intuitive connection with the divine, past lives, spiritual growth.

Angel message: Your guardian angel wants to thank you for being an Earth angel and a bridge to love! You are a lightworker!

White

Aura: Purity, divine thoughts, holiness, positive intentions.

Angel message: Your guardian angel wants you to know that your positive intentions are working. Keep them up!

Silver

Aura: Spiritual protection, archangels, special gifts.

Angel message: Your guardian angel is sending you special gifts. Be aware of coincidences, as they have been synchronized by angels.

Gold

Aura: Prayers, enlightened thoughts, deep connection with the divine, spiritual gifts.

Angel message: Your prayers have been heard and you will soon receive the answers!

Exercise: Looking at your own aura

Looking at your own aura is a great experience. I often do this when I'm lying in bed in the morning. When we've just woken up we're sometimes a little more aware than usual. This is because we're relaxed and have just come from the dream world.

❖ The next time you wake up, raise your hand up above your face and gaze at it.

❖ Look at your middle finger but allow yourself to go into a light dream/trance as you gaze and you'll begin to see your aura developing all around your hand.

❖ Once you've seen this, instantly close your eyes and see what colours swirl in your mind. These are projections of your aura and the angels surrounding you.

Closing your psychic eyes

Switching off your psychic senses is so important. It allows you to retain your energy and not leave yourself vulnerable to wandering energies, particularly when you're asleep.

Exercise: Closing down

To close down your psychic senses you just have to reverse the steps you've already followed to open them:

❖ Close your eyes and see your guardian angel behind you, your golden light of protection all around you.

❖ Then, using the power of your mind, close your third eye. See the eyelid closing over so you switch off your senses.

❖ Then, in your mind, take some time to share your gratitude with the angels for all that you've received.

This last point is quite an important one. Angels *love* being thanked. They absolutely adore it when you take the opportunity to thank them for your experiences with them and all that you've learned.

Being grateful is also a great way to let the universe know you're getting something from a particular experience. Then the universe will provide you with more experiences like it. That's why it's always great to finish every angel experience with thanks!

SUMMARY 🖎

❖ Clairvoyance is the psychic ability to see things beyond the everyday world.

❖ We're all able to perceive angels.

❖ Angels are pure energy but will show themselves in a form to which we can relate.

❖ The aura is the psychic energy that surrounds us.

❖ Our third eye chakra is the key to clairvoyance.

Chapter 10
Hearing angels

'Make yourself familiar with the angels and behold them frequently in spirit; for without being seen, they are present with you.'
ST FRANCIS DE SALES

Hearing angels or tuning in to their voices is probably the most useful psychic sense to develop. Being able to close your eyes and speak inwardly to your angels is beautiful, but to hear a reply is totally awesome. I often just close my eyes and ask the angels for support or their opinion on something and I'll hear a voice say in direct words 'yes' or even 'no', but sometimes it goes beyond a one-word answer and is more loving than words can describe.

'Clairaudience' is the term for being able to hear psychically and it's a wonderful gift. I feel so blessed to have experienced it time and time again in my life. The voice of my guardian angel is so clear that when I allow myself to listen it can have the most life-changing effect.

Taking time to listen

Our angels are speaking to us all of the time. Every time we send a prayer in their direction I truly believe they send a solution back, and often that is through voice. But when our head is filled with the junk of the day or we have the TV on loud or, even more importantly, when we don't believe we're gifted enough to hear angels, we block their divine voices.

Your angels want you to know that you are gifted and that they're with you. They speak to you often and they want you to listen. The first few times you hear them you're bound to be faced with doubt, but when you really do 'listen up' the connection will improve more and more.

Think about the last time you sent your angels a prayer or a request. You sent it up and then left it to them, right? That's absolutely fine. But ask yourself, 'Did I take the time to tune in to the answer?' There's a great chance you didn't.

I'm faced all the time by people saying, 'Why can't I see or hear angels?' or 'How can I improve my connection?' It's simple. Take time to listen. Meditate. Open up. Be present.

Connecting with angels happens now. Not tomorrow, not at the next psychic development class, not when you're on the yoga mat. Your practice is now, it starts this second – let's do it! Every time you put off meditating or tuning in to the voice of your angel, you're stunting your own growth. People often ask why I had it all so young, but the truth of the matter is, I put in the work. Sure, I was a kid and I didn't have as many responsibilities as you, but I meditated every day for at least five minutes. I connected with my angel cards daily. I took every chance to listen.

The voice of your angel will be subtle. It may sound like yours. But, as we discussed earlier, it's not the only way they'll communicate. They'll use anything they can to get through to you – songs, memories or even conversations you hear on television or the radio – and they'll replay the messages in your mind so you can hear them, or share them if you've put in a request on someone else's behalf.

At first when you hear an angel's voice it might seem as though you're imagining it. In fact angels will use your imagination to connect with you. Imagination is wonderful, as we learned in the last chapter, because angels will influence it so we can perceive them.

'What would an angel say or do?'

One technique I always use in my own practice with angels is to think like them. If I'm faced with a challenging decision or question, I ask myself, 'What would an angel say or do?' As angels are complete and utter unconditional love, it's obviously going to be the right decision!

Exercise: Thinking like angels

Take a moment right now to join me in asking yourself some questions:

❖ If you were an angel who could only see love and joy when you looked at this planet and its people, what would you tell yourself right now? Write it down or type it into your phone. Do what you can to get it out.

❖ If your guardian angel had a simple, loving message for you right now, what would it be?

❖ If your angel had three positive keywords for you right now, three words that would help you connect with them, what would they be?

❖ If the angel had a message about a worry, a concern or something that's challenging you right now, what do you think they would tell you to do?

❖ Write down all of these impressions and thoughts. Get them down in black and white. Then read them back over. They will be inspired by the voice of your angel.

How did you get these messages? You may have received impressions, felt a particular way, had a certain thought, heard a voice inside your head, perhaps a voice that waffled a bit to begin with but eventually got to the point... That's your guardian angel communicating through your mind. Hear your angel! Congratulations, you're doing it already! And I believe in you!

Dealing with the ego's promises

Working with angels is brilliant. It really is. The only major hang-up is dealing with the ego. You see not only can the ego make you doubt what you're hearing is true, it can also make false promises. I know first-hand what the ego can do. It can make all kinds of promises and you'll swear you're hearing divine guidance. It's so important that you learn how to spot what's divine guidance and what's the ego trying to pull you into materialism.

I'm not going to lie, my ego has got in the way many times, especially in the early years. One of the greatest promises of the ego is 'Do this and it'll make you rich.' Or it may say, 'Quit your job, move here and I'll make sure your debts are paid.' But it just doesn't work like that. We're all entitled to be entrepreneurs, but putting in the work is a must. And sure angels will come in and push us to take a leap, but they move in baby steps. They aren't interested in materialism and they don't want you to focus solely on material things, but they will help you to be comfortable if you learn the importance of sharing what you have.

Your angels will bring messages that are positive and life-changing, but they won't force you to do anything that's outlandish and crazy. Sometimes their message is so simple and easy that you'll miss it completely. Perhaps because your mind is on other things...? A message I often hear from people is: 'My angels have told me to write a book on healing.' I'm always fascinated and want to hear more. Then when I learn that the person in question is broke, their relationships are falling apart and they've only just learned Reiki, I know it's not the truth. What their angels would really love is for them to help themselves first! If you want to be a big bestselling celebrity author but you've not done the work in your own life, you're not a person of integrity, you're living in an illusionary world. I wouldn't have shared the wisdom and techniques I'm sharing today if I hadn't practised them – what would be the point?

Another message I often hear is: 'My angels have told me to quit my job because I'm surrounded by negative people.' Well, it's wrong! Angels don't believe in calling anyone negative to begin with, they see *everyone* as love. There's a great chance the person making this claim *is* experiencing negativity, however, because 1) they believe it's possible in the first place; 2) they're attracting it through their own thoughts and actions; 3) they have a pattern of leaving one negative workplace and moving into another.

Your angels won't tell you who's negative and who's holding you back because the reality is, you are! But they will believe in you so much that with their help you'll be able to change the most horrible and challenging situation of your life into a positive one. To do so, however, you have to surrender to them and follow their guidance.

The voice of your angel will never judge. It won't tell you to quit, either. It will encourage you to stay put, to focus, to act with love and to believe! When you hear this message, you'll know it's angelic guidance. And when it is time to change something, your angel will show you the way. They'll help you to move forwards, but they'll make sure you're in the right frame of mind first.

When I hear the voices of angels and share their message with people, quite often it's not what they want to hear. They often want me to tell them that they're a special divine person with a sacred mission when the reality is that we *all* have a sacred mission! We're all here to return to love – to *be* love. It's as simple as that. When people want me to say, 'You're going to be a lotto winner, a rock star, a famous personality,' and so on, they're wanting the wrong information. If you have a special gift to share with the world, angels will help you channel it, but they won't show you a shortcut or enable you to push someone out of the way.

This is why it's important to listen intently and discern what's guidance and what's not. Remember not to be duped by the false promises of your ego, because somewhere along the way it's certainly going to make them to you. If the guidance seems challenging, for example 'Send love to your boss' when your boss is giving you a hard time, it probably is divine guidance. The angels want you to focus on love! If the 'divine guidance' is 'Tell your boss she's a psychic vampire' then you know it's your ego talking. That's how you spot the difference. Trust me, you'll catch on quick.

Tuning in to the divine voice

In order to connect with angels we need to tune in to their frequency. I use a visual technique along with meditation to do this. I think of myself as a radio and visualize adjusting my inner dial so that I can tune in to their messages. You can try this later (*see page 126*).

At first, tuning in to the voice of your angels may not be easy, but it will come in time. Clairaudience is like a muscle. When a muscle is unused, it's almost mush. When it's subjected to long hard training sessions, it'll become strong. This is what you need to do to connect with angels: train your psychic muscle so that eventually you can always tune in to their frequency.

My connection to the angels is strong now and I can tune in to it at almost any time. It doesn't always come up with things like people's postcodes or phone numbers, but it does provide simple, heartfelt guidance that helps me stay alert.

Two summers ago I had to tap into my angels' guidance in a way that I'd never done before. I was out with my two best friends, Scott and Teri, at the cinema. We had a brilliant night, but on our way home, around 10 p.m., Scott got an upsetting message on his phone. A boy he'd recently met through mutual friends had texted him while we were at the cinema to say that he'd finished with life and was going to commit suicide.

Scott panicked, as he'd never experienced anything like that before, and decided he was going to call him. By the time he'd called over five times and had no response, he was really worried about the lad's welfare.

Teri also was beginning to worry. 'We all know what he's said... What if he didn't tell anyone else and we were his only contact – the only people who could convince him to stop?'

Looking at his Facebook page, we read, 'Goodbye.' That had been posted over two hours before.

I knew that angels could help, so I decided to meditate. Closing my eyes, I welcomed in their golden light. I felt them nearby and asked them to check on the young man.

They told me clearly, 'He is alive and well. He is sitting at his computer. Send love. There have been no suicide attempts. He will live!'

I told my friends that I trusted my angels more than anyone and that this guidance was clear and direct. I felt as if the lad had been crying out for help, for love and, most of all, for attention. I told them to trust me on it.

The next day the lad was posting on his Facebook page as if nothing had even happened! My friends knew then what I'd heard had been clear and true.

This also showed that angels wouldn't even judge someone who was seeking attention by crying wolf. They'd just deliver the message and leave it with you to decide what happened next. I sent thoughts of love to the young man and I know that he's still alive and well today.

Exercise: Checking in with the angels

You can check in with your angels at any given time, but to get started it may be good to do it in the morning before you start your day or to combine it with your meditation practice. Once you've got the hang of it you can do it at any time.

As it can be challenging initially to trust what you hear, it may be useful to keep a journal nearby or even in your hand as you listen to the messages. By writing down what you hear, or brief bullet points, you'll be able to look back and see how accurate the information was.

Just as with developing our clairvoyance, we can use a technique to open up our channels to hear the voice of our angels. Here's how to do it:

❖ Close your eyes.

❖ Visualize yourself immersed in light.

❖ See your guardian angel standing behind you.

❖ Feel them coming close to you.

❖ At the back of your head, see a radio dial.

❖ Turn this dial with the power of your mind.

❖ See it stop at the word 'angels'.

❖ You are now tuned in to the angels' frequency.

❖ See your ears shining golden light – see it shining right out of them!

❖ Trust the divine wisdom you hear.

❖ Say, 'Thank you for revealing to me what I need to know, my angels!'

❖ Focus on your breath and listen intently. You can keep your eyes closed or open as you do so. Write down everything you hear.

❖ You may also want to ask questions such as 'What's the next step?' or, thinking about a particular concern, 'Is this the right step for me?' Trust what comes through.

❖ If you struggle to hear anything at all, focus on your loving centre and feel the angels coming close to you. If they were to speak to you right now, what would they say? What do you feel their guidance would be? If they were to use your imagination to communicate with you right now, what would they say? Trust it!

❖ To disconnect, thank your angels for all you have received.

❖ See the light in your ears dimming.

❖ Visualize the radio dial turning to 'off'.

❖ See roots coming from your feet, penetrating the ground and going deep into the Earth's core.

❖ Open your eyes.

Checking in with a friend

When you're developing your psychic skills, having a like-minded friend you can check in with is definitely a good idea. Maybe you're developing your skills at the same time as someone you know or, even better, you have someone available who's a little bit more experienced than you are. If you're having trouble trusting your guidance or you're unsure what you're hearing is correct, why not confide in someone you can trust?

I am glad to have many like-minded friends and a particularly psychic mother with whom I can discuss specific guidance. I often hear something and double-check with my psychic friend Diane, or she will call and ask me something. This gives me the opportunity to ensure I am working towards my own highest good and that of those around me. It's a great system to have set up.

Signs

Another great way to know if what you're hearing is from your angels is to ask them for a sign. When they send you a reminder of their presence not long after you have received some guidance, it's their way of saying that what you have heard is right.

Sometimes you don't need to ask for a sign, though, because they'll send you so many of them once you start trusting and following their guidance! Recently they sent me a sign when I was on business in London. I'd been unsure about going on a two-hour train journey to a town I hadn't ever visited to do a show. I had a cold, I was tired and I just wanted to go home. In the back of my mind I could hear myself saying, 'Don't let anyone down, Kyle.' At that moment I checked in with my angels and I heard, 'Go to the show. It will be a blessing.' So I decided to go.

I was early for my train, so thought I'd go and have a coffee while waiting. I went in and ordered my favourite drink and as I did so I noticed the name badge of the guy serving me had 'Angel' written on it in large letters. I knew then everything was going to be wonderful.

That night I was standing in front of 200 people in a small town in the south of England. One of the messages that came through was relayed by the same voice that I'd heard that day at the station. I heard it say, 'We are here to speak to the woman who has lost three children.' As I looked up from where I was standing on the left-hand side of the audience, I shared the message in full: that I would be standing directly in front of a woman who had had pregnancy issues, in particular losing three children.

A woman three rows back from where I was standing waved at me. She could understand the message.

As I looked at her, an angel appeared, a female angel dressed in pure pearly-whites. She had long flowing blonde hair and was like an angel straight out of a movie. As I looked at her, I heard clearly, 'A new child is on the way. He has tried many times to come to this worthy mother. We angels want her to know that everything is safe and well. Please let her know.'

I passed the words over the audience verbatim and many of us were moved to tears.

The lady was so grateful and happy. She then stood up and said, 'This is so true. I have had many challenges having children and we gave up on having any more. I love the two that are with me now. But I have something to share. My friends who are with me don't even know. I'm eight weeks pregnant!'

The whole audience went into uproar and applauded. It was amazing to see. I asked them all to close their eyes with me as I prayed for a positive, uplifting pregnancy for the lady, who the angels knew was a worthy and deserving mother. What a miracle! It was a blessed experience, just as I'd been told.

Exercise: Channelling angel messages for a friend

After practising checking in and connecting with the angels for yourself, it's a beautiful thing to tune in for a friend. Offering your newfound love and support from the angels to a friend is a unique experience. Not only does it give you some more experience in 'checking in', but it allows you to share. Angels love it when we share. Also, when we perform an act of service for another person, it lights up that person's world and creates a wave of kindness, and this wave carries so much love into their life and the lives of those surrounding them.

◆ Arrange to have some private time with your friend. Ensure you have a pen and paper handy just in case you want to note anything you hear or receive.

◆ Take the hands of your friend and close your eyes.

◆ Thank the angels for being present.

◆ Imagine a golden light swirling above and washing over you both.

◆ See your radio dial moving to 'angels'.

◆ Simply think, *If the angels had a message for [friend's name], it would be...* then trust what comes through.

❖ You can listen to the message then tell them what you heard or give them the message word by word. You may even stop every now and then to write down what you have received and then share it.

❖ Then ask the angels for three keywords you can share with your friend. You may hear words such as 'peace', 'love', 'balance', 'prioritize', 'go for it', 'believe' and so on. Share what you feel these words could mean to your friend.

❖ After this you could ask in your mind any questions that your friend has for the angels. See how you get on. This may take some time, but at least try!

❖ When you've finished, ask for feedback.

❖ Thank the angels and close down.

SUMMARY

❖ Every time we ask for help, an angel is already whispering the solution to us.

❖ We can check in with the angels to ensure an experience is right for us.

❖ Angels will use all forms of audio to communicate with us.

❖ When we follow our guidance, signs will bless our path.

❖ Angels love it when we share.

Chapter 11
Feeling angels

*'The guardian angels of life sometimes
fly so high as to be beyond our sight, but
they are always looking down upon us.'*

JEAN-PAUL RICHTER, WRITER

Have you ever just known something and had no idea why? My mother likes to say, 'I can feel it in my water.' Wherever you feel it, you'll know that feeling when you walk into a room and just know some sort of hostile drama has taken place. Or when you walk into a room where everyone is smiling and celebrating and you can't help but join in...

The ability to feel emotions, angels and spirit is called 'clairsentience' and it means 'clear-feeling'. Many people say that there's a fourth psychic sense of 'knowing', but I truly feel that it can be bracketed with clairsentience.

Clairsentience comes very easily when our energy and emotions are clear. When we're tainted by past challenges, grievances and grudges, however, they stand between us and our ability to feel the energy that surrounds us.

Feeling the presence of angels is the most indescribable divine experience. I have this feeling installed permanently in my life and it's absolutely beautiful. Deep within the core of my belly I have the sensation that there is more energy surrounding me than the human senses can understand.

It is a feeling that goes beyond the body, but it can really hit us in our tummy. I believe clairsentience relates to our heart and our solar plexus. We all know what it's like having a 'gut feeling' and this is exactly what this is: a sense of connection to our heart and soul in order to perceive the energy of a situation.

Feeling the energy of your angels is a training of the mind, it's focusing your faith and trusting that they are with you and allowing that feeling of trust to guide you to the next step. You can, however, feel with your hands too.

Working with your hands to feel

I use angel cards in my daily practice and I believe that the angels will encourage me to pick the cards that are right for me by allowing me to feel them. I teach this as part of my angel cards reading course. What I'll do is encourage the group to practise holding their left hand (the hand closest to the heart) over the deck to see if they feel a draught, tingle or sensation that makes them want to stop. Wherever they stop is where they have to pick the card.

Earlier in the book we learned how to give a friend an angel healing through our hands and I hope that you've already been able to do this, as it just allows you to get more of an idea of the feeling experience.

Your hands are powerful and they tell your story. If you look at someone as they speak, they generally use their hands in some way or another. Our hands can feel, they can heal and they connect us directly to the heart. Holding hands is an act of love, married couples wear rings on their hands to signify their love and people bite the nails on their hands when they're nervous. Hands are a beautiful part of the body and they fascinate me.

I've noticed we can use our hands to feel our own aura and they can also help us feel someone else's story, emotions and angelic guidance. You can also ask your guardian angel to let you feel their subtle energy through your hands. Here are some exercises to try.

Exercise: Feeling the aura

❖ Rub your hands together for a good minute to sensitize them.

❖ Lift them into the air, level with your shoulders, palms facing each other.

❖ Allow yourself to experience the energy and tingles or any other sensation you feel between your hands.

❖ Bring your hands together at your heart centre and move them back and forth towards each other but don't allow them to touch.

- ❖ Become aware of the energy that you are gliding through, touching and feeling.

- ❖ Now close your eyes and continue moving your palms in and out towards each other.

- ❖ Take your hands away but imagine they are still moving in and out. Feel that energy – allow it to go beyond the physical.

- ❖ Then, in your heart, know that everything surrounding you is energy. You are energy and your friends, family, pets and home are filled with energy.

- ❖ Take some time to feel the energy all around you, using your internal senses.

Feeling someone's energy and emotions

I've found it's easier to tap into others' energy in order to bring them guidance from angels, and if you can get the knack for them, you have it for yourself too. In many ways this whole book has led to you being able to tune in for yourself and others – and this is the best way to learn, by practising on all levels possible.

If you give someone else guidance and you're not following the guidance given to you, though, you're not in the right space to develop further. Only pass on guidance to someone else if you're following your own – it's only fair.

A true spiritual channel is a person of integrity. So, throw your hands up if you don't know the answer and live your talk. If you tell someone to do something and don't follow it yourself, you're kidding yourself on so much that you'll end up stunting your growth.

With this in mind, you can now take feeling with your hands to the next level: you can tap into someone else's energy and feel how they feel. This is one of the nicest things to do because you facilitate a space for someone to discuss their emotions in a safe and positive environment.

Exercise: Feeling

With a partner, go somewhere where you'll not be disturbed. Explain to them that you're developing your skills and promise nothing but honesty.

Before you connect for them it's important to put a light of protection on, so visualize yourself bathed in a golden light and see your guardian angel standing behind you in your mind.

❖ Once you've done this, open your eyes and take the hands of your partner.

❖ Ask them simply, 'Can I have your permission to feel your emotions, heart and angel, please?'

❖ When they say, 'Yes,' then say mentally something along the lines of 'Thank you, angel of [person's name] for drawing close to me and allowing me to feel and understand their emotions and any messages you have for them.'

❖ Then, closing your eyes, just focus on your breath and breathe. Anything you feel, just say it. Tell the person every thought you think and every emotion you feel. If you just suddenly know something, tell them.

❖ Next, feel with your heart what the angel wants to convey to the person. Do you feel love, harmony, peace, healing energy? Tell them what you're receiving.

❖ It's good to close your eyes, get a piece of information, share it, then start again and keep going.

❖ When you feel you've come to the end, ask for feedback and if the person has any questions.

❖ If a question is asked, just say it in your mind to the angel and feel for an answer. You might just get a good feeling or you might feel weird. That's fine. Just tell the person everything.

❖ Thank the angel internally and then imagine a sword coming down, separating your energy from the other person's.

❖ Drink some water to ground yourself.

Your 'feeling' centre

It may take a while for you to master feeling from the inside. Starting with the hands is best. One day it all just fell into place for me. I think it was because I have a vivid imagination and I could visualize what something would look like and feel like in my mind. And when I shared it, it was always accurate.

The solar plexus chakra, the gut, is so strong. This is where I believe all feeling comes from. It's the centre that governs our willpower, our assertiveness and our get up and go.

I've noticed that if this energy centre is out of balance it can affect our ability to feel properly, so it's important to balance it. You'll know if your solar plexus is out of balance because physical or mental challenges will be present in your life. Your sleeping patterns will generally be all over the place, you may be bingeing on foods that are heavy, you'll be tired, your mind will be overthinking all of the time, you'll be afraid of the next step in your life and you'll feel as though you need to be in control of the plans for the day ahead. You could also have digestive issues, feel bloated or bagged up or have uncontrollable frustration/anger.

It won't do you any harm right now to ensure your solar plexus centre is in balance. I love doing this simply because I love the sunshine. Sunshine? Well, as the solar plexus makes reference to solar energy, what better energy to use to balance this centre than the sun?

Exercise: Drawing down the sun

❖ Sit cross-legged on the floor with your back straight, or in a chair with your feet on the ground.

❖ Visualize the sun shining brightly above you.

❖ Allow its light to bathe your whole body in positive energy.

❖ Thank the sun for being there and being your energy source.

❖ Visualize it coming closer and closer to your body.

❖ Finally, it gets so close it becomes one with your body.

- ❖ It moves down your head, face, chin and neck.

- ❖ It keeps moving down your chest, past your heart.

- ❖ It rests just above your navel.

- ❖ Its light shines out brightly from the core of your stomach.

- ❖ Your solar plexus is now balanced with light and energy.

- ❖ Use the affirmation: 'I am filled with the light of the sun. I am light!'

Opening your heart centre

As angels are divine beings of love, it's so important you make your energy available to that essence. Your heart centre is the space that's connected to your capacity to give and receive love and I believe that angels use this space so we can tap into their loving guidance and support.

If you've had challenges with letting love in, the next exercise will help you. It encourages angelic healing in the place that matters most so that you can really tap into love as an energy and allow it to bloom in your life. Knowing about angels and their love for you may already have had a healing effect on your life, but when you allow them into your heart, guidance remains there for you.

I believe that connecting with angels is a sort of initiation. It's giving permission for them to connect with you and bless your heart with their divine healing rays. By allowing them into your heart, you are handing them your trust and issuing a spiritual invitation for them to unfold their miracles in your life. Opening up your heart can not only help you with your spiritual development but also bring positive shifts in your personal life.

If you've been hurt or let down in the past, there's a good chance that you've allowed a barrier to go up around your heart. This can not only be an obstruction to angelic help but to letting in love at all. When angels come close to you, they'll encourage you to open your heart and feel again. It's a beautiful thing to be able to let love in, because it's absolutely what you deserve.

Now is the time to open up that heart of yours so that you can feel your angel close to you.

Exercise: Opening your heart

✦ Say this prayer:

> *Thank you, angels, for removing the barriers that surround my heart. I am now ready and open to receive your love and support. As my heart opens, I balance myself, I welcome love in and share love in an effortless way. I recognize that love is who I am and the purpose of my being. I am open and receptive to loving experiences from now on. And so it is.*

✦ Place your hands upon your heart with your right hand overlapping your left.

✦ Close your eyes and breathe towards your hands.

✦ As you do so, allow yourself to relax and feel your heart.

- ❖ Visualize healing emerald light flowing from heaven through your head and into your heart centre.

- ❖ See this light going through every area of your heart and cleaning out any old resentment, fear or grievances you're holding there.

- ❖ Visualize the light touching the barriers of your heart and breaking through them so that they are removed.

- ❖ As the barriers are removed, an angel appears before you. They wrap their arms and wings all around you and pour the love of their being into you.

- ❖ Allow yourself to accept this healing, this love, this light that helps you perceive the world in a different and completely positive way.

- ❖ When you're ready, thank the angel and open your eyes.

Inviting your angel to come close to you

In order for you to feel your angel's presence you must invite them to come close to you. It is all about being in the right frame of mind and having a balanced energy that will really allow that experience to develop.

There's something so comforting about knowing your angel is there. By now you should have got an idea of who your angel is, how they look and hopefully even how they speak to you. Now you have to bring all of these aspects together and use all your psychic senses to get an idea of how it feels when your angel is nearby.

It helps to continue practising the different exercises we've been through so far and if you can work on your skills with a partner or group of friends and gain feedback and support, all the better.

You can draw your angel close to you in a number of ways. I prefer to use prayer and meditation to really allow their energy to unite with mine. Here's a candle ritual.

Exercise: A candle ritual to welcome your guardian angel close to you

Candles are magical. I've always believed that when we light a candle while setting an intention or saying a prayer, the flame carries the energy of that thought until it burns out.

Candles have always had a close connection with psychic powers and clairvoyance, so I thought it would be a lovely experience for you to light a candle and meditate in front of it so you can work on developing your spiritual senses and draw your angel close to you at the same time.

You'll need a candle, of course. Any will do, but I recommend having a large pillar candle or a stick candle level with your eyes so you can gaze directly into it. If that's going to be an issue, you can gaze down into a tea light if need be.

❖ Turn most of the lights out and have the candle sitting safely on a fireproof dish in front of you. I prefer to gaze at a candle on my altar and sit cross-legged in front of it. Note: If you blink while gazing, this is OK. Just bring your attention back to the flame.

- ✦ Gaze at the candle flame and allow its golden light to wash over you.

- ✦ In your mind, set the intention that you want to draw your angel close to you.

- ✦ Feel in your heart and in your soul that they are enveloping you in their energy.

- ✦ Keep gazing at the candle and visualize your third eye centre opening up.

- ✦ As your third eye opens, feel yourself attune to the vision of your angel.

- ✦ See yourself tapping into the voice of your angel as you gaze towards the candle.

- ✦ Feel, see and hear their presence.

- ✦ Breathing steadily and deeply through both nostrils, allow yourself to go into a light trance.

- ✦ When your gaze has become a stare, close your eyes immediately.

- ✦ Pay attention to the thoughts, messages, words or impressions that come to you.

- ✦ Then say a quiet prayer like 'Thank you, angel. I am so glad you are close to me. I allow you into my heart. Thank you for staying there!'

- ✦ Place your hands on the ground at either side of your body and press firmly down to ground yourself.

- ✦ Drink some water and maybe eat some nuts or fruit to ground yourself.

Eventually it will become automatic for you to direct your energy and focus to your angel in order to feel them around you, and a beautiful feeling of safety and support will come to you in return.

SUMMARY 🖎

◆ Clairsentience is the gift of feeling.

◆ Feeling others' emotions helps us understand feeling energy.

◆ Feeling with our hands helps us develop the idea of feeling inside.

◆ Our heart and solar plexus are the centres where we feel.

◆ We can draw our angel close to us and feel their energy.

Chapter 12
Building the bridge

*'Your newborn purpose is nursed by
angels, cherished by the Holy Spirit
and protected by God himself.'*

A Course in Miracles

Now it's time to build a bridge to your angels. This will enable you to open up to their guidance on every level.

Powerful prayers

Prayer is the bridge that enables you to speak to angels. It's the medium of miracles that allows you to send your thoughts, thanks and intentions to heaven. Prayer is our candid conversation with our guardians. It's the moment we choose to connect. I believe that when we pray we create an altar in our minds where we can commune with the divine. We raise our vibes and draw the golden light of the angels to us like a magnet.

Prayer is speaking to heaven. It's an open call. It's a conference call to heaven. God, the angels and our loved ones up there begin to hear our thoughts and our requests. It is through prayer that we can ask for help; it is through prayer that we can open up to that help and all the abundance that is there for us.

If you want to create a strong and divine connection to your angel guides it's important that you pray to them often and thank them for being close to you. It is through my daily prayer practice that I've discovered the true power of my angels.

Vibration

Everything in the universe is energy and energy itself is a vibration. On Earth our energy is of a lower frequency than that of angels and the spirit world, so when we want to connect with their energy we must raise our vibration. This is why many people don't have spiritual experiences when they want – it's down to the vibration of their energy at that time. Your aim as a spiritual being living in a human world is to keep your energy high. But we all know what it's like to be low and drained ... don't we?

Think about a time when you've tried a spiritual technique, maybe one in this book or another book that's out there. You've followed some of the instructions and are enjoying the process, but one of your family members keeps banging about downstairs and it's putting you off. You try to stay focused, but you can feel the blood boil to your head and you shout, *'Be quiet, I'm trying to meditate here!'* Then you try and get back into your practice but you're just not successful at all...

The reason for this is that when we get frustrated, angry or annoyed, we lower our vibration. The angelic realm is of a much higher vibration than ours to begin with and to stay connected to it we must learn to hold our vibration and our intentions in the busiest of places. It's all down to being able to find a sense of contentment and inner peace wherever we are.

I learned how to do this while spending time in London. By sitting in the park and meditating and praying with my eyes closed I learned to let all the world around me just be. When I stopped worrying about the sirens, noises and other distractions, I realized I could open up to my angelic guidance system. Perfect!

Raising the vibes

Raising your vibration to heaven is a lot simpler than you think. It's just a matter of aligning yourself with love. How you do it is up to you. But having a set of mindsets, intentions, images, affirmations and thoughts can help.

Safety thought

As the spiritual laws encourage us to know that whatever we think about we create, or whatever we feel affects the next step, it's important to have some thought we can turn to and rely on. I love having a thought that makes me feel safe.

My safety thought is simple: whenever I'm overwhelmed, emotional or stressed out about something, I think about sunflowers. I often think about the famous sunflower painting by Vincent van Gogh and recreate it in my mind. Sometimes I think about a sunflower standing tall in a field. In the centre of the sunflower is a happy smiley face and it's nodding in a gentle breeze. By the time I've finished thinking about the sunflower, I'm happy again.

The sunflower has since become my 'spiritual symbol'. I even bought my last office because of it. When I was searching for a space that was perfect for me I found one with a sunflower carved into the cornice of the roof! I knew then it was for me.

You can create your own safety thought to keep yourself aligned with love and you can use it in a host of different ways. For example, if you're giving an angel reading to a friend and you're confused or mixed up, you can focus on your safety thought to realign yourself. Another great way to use your safety thought is when you're thinking the worst about a situation or becoming distracted during a meditation. A safety thought is just great, especially if it's something you love and is personal to you. Past students of mine have had a whole variety of safety thoughts. Here's a selection:

- a childhood memory

- the image of your child

- a family member you adore

- a giant love heart

◆   your favourite deity (such as Ganesha, the Indian elephant god who removes obstacles)

◆   your favourite colour in the shape of a diamond or triangle

Positive affirmations

Positive affirmations are a wonderful way to keep your energy high. Affirmations are declarations. They are statements you make in order to create something. They can be based on where you are now and the blessings you have already, but they can also bring awesome states of being. They are the first step to creating a life you love. Start saying them, even if you can't believe in them yet. Eventually you will and, I promise, then you will see! I have given a selection of affirmations at the end of the book (*see page 167*), but in the meantime, let's take a moment to say this extended affirmation:

> *I am love. I am the universe. I am united with my angels and it feels great. My body, mind and soul are one, connected to everything that is and ever will be. I support myself, I am supported by God and I surrender to the loving energy that surrounds me. I am surrounded by people who reflect my energy. I am harmonious, at peace and serene. Light fills my body. It is well, I am well and I share this with the world. I am blessed to be on this journey! What a pleasure life is. Thank you, universe, thank you!*

Taking a second to change the way you think can change your world, and it can help you perceive the love and support of your angels too. When we are feeling low it's as though we shut off heaven and its help. When we take a moment to believe in angels, to know they are there, to affirm it with our thoughts, intentions, words and actions, we align with them, we raise our vibes and we become a bridge to the light that surrounds us.

The 'I am' energy

Every time you say 'I am' and then a word, particularly a word connected with an emotion, the universe hears you and aligns you with the energy of that word. So, if you say, 'I am lonely,' your energy becomes a magnet for loneliness. Whereas when you say, 'I am so blessed,' *and mean it*, you welcome, attract and draw even more blessings into your life.

Every time you say 'I am...' be *aware* of your thoughts, your emotions and what you're about to attract into your life. Intention is everything and it's time to intend the best. When you're aware of the greatness of your life, your power and your energy, it extends your awareness to the angels, to God and to the universal life-force that you are.

Meditation

If prayer is speaking, meditating is listening. Every time you take a moment to meditate, you're giving your angels another opportunity to share.

Meditation aligns you with love. It lifts your energy. You don't only raise your vibration, you vibrate complete love.

Meditation is the most powerful tool in developing a connection with your angels. You don't even have to go anywhere or listen to a guided CD or visualize yourself in paradise. You can simply close your eyes, focus on your breath and just simply let go – while remembering the few points outlined below.

Dealing with the ego and doubt in meditation

The ego. That inner doubt system can get in the way of your divine voice, your angels and your guides. It's not always easy to overcome it, but here are a few techniques that have helped me get in touch with myself so I can tune in to the angels again.

Relax

It's important to relax. The best way to do this is by focusing on your breath and not tensing up your body.

Let go

When you meditate there's a great chance you may want to cough, sneeze, cry – who knows what? Don't hold it in. Let it out.

Affirmation

Try this affirmation:

> *It's safe for me to enjoy this experience.*

Mudras

There are two mudras (yoga hand locks) that we will use to support our meditations.

◆ Jnana Mudra: The traditional meditation finger pose where you create an 'OK' sign with your fingers and allow your palms to face upwards.

◆ Fist: By bringing your hands from Jnana Mudra into a fist you allow yourself to connect with the five spiritual elements and realign your energy.

Don't hate, meditate!

The 'H' word is such a strong one. It is a negative word that is fear-based. When I think about what 'hate' looks like I see hot black tar clinging onto my skin, and it's not supposed to be there. The word is so commonly used in this world, but I avoid it because I don't want to be that word. Whenever I hear someone say 'I hate' I've got into the routine of asking them to tell me what they *love*.

Being aware of your words is so important. We can change our intentions, but we need to put at least five positive things in place to cancel out, let go of and delete our initial intention.

Exercise: 'I love...'

❖ The next time you hear yourself say 'I hate...', close your eyes and become aware.

❖ Then meditate on something you love.

❖ Meditate on five things you love.

This will change your thoughts and intentions and help you focus on what you have, not on what you don't have or dislike!

SUMMARY 📣

❖ The universe is energy.

❖ To connect with the angels we must raise our vibration.

❖ Prayer is a powerful way to connect.

❖ Meditation is the ultimate tool for listening.

❖ An affirmation is a declaration that creates the next step on our path.

Chapter 13
Angelic toolbox

*'An angel can illuminate our thoughts and
minds by strengthening the power of vision.'*
ST THOMAS AQUINAS

In order to open up to angels we need a spiritual toolkit.
This includes asking for protection, tuning in and out,
receiving guidance, cleansing our energy and balancing
our senses.

Psychic protection

Protecting our energy is vital in any spiritual development
work. When we open up, we open up to all the energy
that's moving around us and sometimes there will
be challenging energy to face. Have you ever been in
a space where there has been an argument or people
aren't getting on? You sit there for as long as possible,
but you feel your head getting heavy and sore and you
become tired and drained. That's what it's like to face
challenging energy.

People can be draining too. You'll probably already be aware of that, especially if you spend a lot of time with the general public or those who are particularly needy. I'm sure you know what it's like to deal with someone who keeps going on and on about their life, their past, their relationship problems, their financial worries and so on. If you've been there, you'll certainly know what it's like to feel drained...

So, the first thing you must do before you conduct any psychic or spiritual work is create an energy of protection. We did it earlier by visualizing a golden light surrounding us and I've come up with even more techniques you can use. You can even make up your own. Whatever it is, if it makes you feel safe and protected then it will most definitely work.

Visualize a golden cloak

One of the techniques I use is to imagine myself wearing a golden cloak. I allow the golden light to surround my whole body and I even bring up my hood if I need to so that I know I'm safe and protected.

Visualize swords surrounding you

This is my *ultimate* protection ritual. I use this if I'm dealing with challenging people, TV companies or even larger audiences or book signings. It's quite simple: I visualize swords surrounding me facing outwards. I don't just imagine one or two – I'm talking 20 or more and I see them floating and swirling all around me. Whenever any challenging or negative energy comes close, the swords cut it down.

Visualize a sheet of steel

Trying to disconnect from a challenging person is never easy, especially if you can feel them draining you emotionally. I always find at book launches and signings there are one or two people who stand overwhelmingly close to me. I always do my best to step back, but when people step closer again I do this to change things: I visualize a huge sheet of steel falling between us, just like you see in the movies when someone tries to rob the bank and a big screen comes down in front of the cashier to protect them. I allow the sheet to protect me and disconnect my energy from whoever is challenging me. It works every time. Sometimes, as it happens I'll even say in my mind 'I am free.'

Archangel Michael protection prayer

Archangel Michael will probably become one of your greatest friends if you get into this angel stuff. You can call on him at any point to bring you safety and protection. Use this protection prayer at the start of your day or even carry it on a piece of paper so you can tap into his strength at any time.

Thank you, Archangel Michael, for surrounding me with your protective light and strength. I am safe and protected, shielded and strong. It feels so good to know you're at my back.

And so it is!

Cutting the cords

I mentioned cutting the cords earlier. When we cut the cords, we release, disconnect from and let go of any harsh energy, emotional ties and blockages that are getting in the way of our inner peace.

Cutting the cords is easy, but it can also be extremely emotional. When we're emotionally and spiritually freed from a tie that has been holding us back it can be a huge relief for our heart and soul.

Exercise: Cord-cutting

To cut the cords you must be able to stay relaxed and present in meditation.

The process is very simple:

❖ Visualize yourself bathed in a golden light of protection.

❖ In your mind, allow yourself to become aware of any blockages, ties or situations of your past that you feel are standing between you and peace.

❖ Allow these situations, people and places to become ribbons wrapping tightly round you.

❖ In your mind, see a beautiful golden angel coming towards you with a huge sword of light in their hand.

❖ As soon as the sword touches a ribbon, the ribbon disintegrates. See the sword cutting through all of the ribbons. The cords are cut. You are released. You are free.

❖ Take some time to feel the power of your freedom.

❖ Thank the angel and open your eyes.

❖ To finish the cord-cutting ceremony, say this prayer:

> *Thank you, angels and Archangel Michael, for cutting the cords that bind me to people, places and situations. I am safe and free! And so it is!*

Cleansing the energy

There will be times when you feel your energy needs a good steep, but that's OK! When we open up to angels we're always connected to love, but the vibes of the people we connect with in life can be influential and make us feel down.

I do readings as my full-time job, and sometimes after a long day I can feel tired and drained. Sometimes it's not even due to negative energy, sometimes it's just low energy. I have come to realize that looking after my body, mind and soul is very important and I do different rituals for them all.

Salt baths

I love baths! They're all brilliant, but there's one type of bath that can really adjust and cleanse your energy: sea salt baths! That's right, having a nice relaxing bath with sea salts can have the most amazing effect. One of my dear psychic friends, Diane Etherson, has Dead Sea salt baths all the time. She goes through bags of the stuff to ensure her energy and chakras are 'blinging', as she would say. My personal favourite is Himalayan salt. I love a Himalayan salt bath – it always revitalizes me.

Exercise

Exercise definitely gets your spirit aligned. For many years my body was so out of shape that when I began to be aware of it and exercise more, things really did shift. There's no particular style of exercise I can recommend, but I can say that you need to make the effort with it – no half-assed stuff. Get moving and feel your spirit align!

Yoga

Yoga has been my ultimate life-saver. It's allowed me to get focused, not only on my body and breath, but on God too. When I go onto my mat I can feel my angels circle around me. I've even seen angels supporting and loving the people they are looking after when I've been to public classes.

Yoga unites the body, mind and soul and this helps us with angelic development because we become more aware, and really that's what's missing when we don't experience these beings. I enjoy the more dynamic Ashtanga classes, as there's no way you can be distracted when you're doing so much focusing on your body, alignment, breath and moving to the next posture.

Sage smudging

Sage sticks are available in most spiritual shops. This Native American technique is a highly recommended way to cleanse your aura and chakras. All you do is light the sage (white sage is the best) and allow it to burn. Then, using a large feather, fan or even your hand, you direct the smoke around your aura from head to toe.

I've found that doing this for yourself can be challenging, so it's also a great way to connect with a partner. You cleanse their vibes and they do yours in return. I love doing this and have done it at the beginning of workshops. It's always fun too!

Tuning in

Tuning in is what you should do as you connect with your angel or the angel of another person. It's the process you go through to raise your energy, open up your psychic senses and give your angels permission to communicate. Tuning in ultimately creates the bridge between you and the angelic realm. I tune in at the beginning of my meditation practice, when I'm reading angel cards for myself or another person, or when I'm doing some sort of public speaking. It's my way of being an open channel to love and the angels.

You've already tuned in throughout the book in different ways. You've opened up your third eye, your ears and of course the feeling centres of the heart and solar plexus. The following process brings all of these together and opens them up as one. You can use it if it feels right to you or you can create your own way of tuning in. Whatever makes you think 'I'm in' is the best way for you.

Exercise: Tuning in

❖ Closing your eyes, visualize golden light above you.

❖ See the light washing over all of your being.

❖ Visualize your guardian angel standing behind you, their wings wrapping you in a light of protection.

❖ Visualize your heart opening up and frequencies of love pouring out and in.

❖ See your solar plexus lighting up like the sun's energy, representing your positive intentions and willpower.

❖ At the back of your head, visualize a radio dial turning until it reaches 'angels'.

❖ See your ears pour light out as a representation of hearing the angels speak.

❖ In the middle of your brows, visualize an eye opening and shining brightly.

❖ Allow yourself to connect with angels.

❖ At this point you can request guidance, go on your meditation practice or connect for someone else. Allow it to flow.

Tuning out

Just as tuning in is important to establish a connection, tuning out is too. It ensures you don't leave yourself wide open to the emotions, energy and information that are floating around everywhere. It's an act of self-love. I make sure I do it every day and if I forget, I'll do it before bed.

Exercise: Tuning out

To tune out, just reverse the steps as follows:

❖ See the third eye centre closing over and fading away.

❖ Visualize your heart closing over – not fully, but enough to prevent you feeling too many frequencies.

❖ See the radio dial at the back of your head turning until it clicks onto 'off'.

❖ Thank your angels, thank God and thank the universe for all that you have received.

❖ See roots coming from your feet, penetrating the ground and going deep into the Earth's core.

❖ Open your eyes and connect with your surroundings.

SUMMARY 🖎

❖ It's important to use psychic protection to keep yourself safe.

❖ Cleansing your energy keeps your channels open and clear.

❖ Exercise and yoga keep your energy open and receptive.

❖ Having a healthy body helps you have a healthy spiritual practice.

Prayers and affirmations

Creating positive energy on a daily basis and welcoming your angels in through affirmation and prayer is the best way to nurture the bond you've formed with your angels. Ensuring that your energy is focused on love, that you've given the angels permission to be present on your path and that you're open to their guidance is a wonderful experience.

My favourite author, Louise Hay, says that we live our day by the way we start it and that really is true. When we welcome the angels at the beginning of our day and open up to them, we allow them to live our day with us.

At the start of each day I welcome the angels in. I speak to them on my way to the office and all through the day. I thank them for getting me through traffic, keeping me safe and helping me to work with pure love and integrity in my heart. It's my pleasure to share with you a selection of angel prayers and affirmations that you can use to develop your connection with them.

Prayers

A morning prayer

Good morning, dear angels.

Thank you for keeping me safe.

It feels so good to start this day with you, knowing that there is a peace deep within my heart that is being reflected back to me throughout my day.

Thank you for reminding me of your presence and sending your support.

By the grace of God I am blessed, knowing I travel this pathway with you, my friends!

And so it is!

A prayer for clairvoyance

Thank you, dear angels, for awakening my sight so I can clearly see and sense you.

I allow you to open my energy so I can perceive nothing but the truth and the loving energy that surrounds me.

I align myself with love and peace and allow my energy to be raised to yours!

I am pleased and blessed to see you, and my eyes are open.

And so it is!

Surrendering the day

Dear universe and angels, I surrender my day to you, knowing only good things are happening now and only peaceful experiences are before me.

And so it is!

A prayer for healing

Thank you, healing angels, for washing your rays over my entire being.

I am blessed knowing that the divine physician has placed his hands upon me and sent his legion of angels to return me to health.

I am safe, strong and well!

And so it is!

An evening prayer

Thank you, divine angels, for surrounding me now as I prepare to sleep.

Thank you for removing any energy that doesn't need to be here as I make space for a deep, pleasant slumber that returns my body and energy to natural balance.

I feel safe knowing you protect me as I sleep.

May the world be blessed by your light.

And so it is.

Affirmations

The doors are always open in my career, with angels leading the way!

I am surrounded by angels and Earth angels alike. It's bliss!

My health is my wealth. Healing angels have blessed my body, mind and soul! I am safe.

I am protected by the light and love of angels!

Angels stand before me, beside me and behind me. Only love can surpass their light!

I allow the energy of my heart to open as I allow the angels of romance to direct my love life!

Questions and answers

For the curious, here is a selection of frequently asked questions on angels.

If angels exist, do bad or fallen angels exist too?

I'm often asked if 'fallen angels' exist and my answer is always a definite 'no'. They are mentioned in religious texts, but I've yet to have an experience of an angel who's fallen from grace. In order to believe in fallen angels we have to believe in the existence of evil and I believe there is only love or fear. Eternal love is my focus. If you believe in evil, you can in turn create evil experiences, but the truth of the matter is it is nothing but an illusion. Angels exist, fallen angels do not.

Did my angel know me in a previous life?

If you've had a previous life, your angel most definitely would have watched over you then. I believe before we even come into our present existence our soul bonded with our angel. That is why connecting with them is such a beautifully familiar experience. It's almost our soul's way of saying 'I remember.'

Can angels leave you?

Your guardian angel can never leave you and it doesn't matter how bad you think you are or what choices you've made in your life, they'll be with you. If they can't get you away from a challenging situation, they'll support you through it.

Do we draw angels closer to us by reading about them?

When we read about angels, we *absolutely* draw them closer to us. When we keep seeing the word 'angels' and they hear us read it in our mind or out loud, they will always be drawn to us. I have heard hundreds of stories about people having angel experiences while reading my books, particularly my first book, *The Angel Whisperer*. Many people said they could see a blue light coming out of the pages and one woman wrote to me to say that hers produced feathers. They'd just keep coming out of the pages. Wow!

When you get a white feather from your angel are you meant to keep it?

Many people like to keep these feathers but there'll come a point, after being into angels for a while, where you'll run out of space. I always just take the time to say, 'Thank you, angels, for this amazing sign,' and then let the feather go. You can keep significant ones if you want. The feather that fell out of the book I read all those years ago is still in there. The angels don't want us to be too attached to material things, though – that's why it's OK to let their feathers go.

Can we have more than one particular angel?

We are all given one guardian angel, but that doesn't mean we can't have two. There's always more than one angelic guide working with us and I've sometimes seen two or three with my clients. It is important to keep things simple and build a relationship with one guide at a time, but others will reveal themselves to you as they work with you.

Angels who help you with a particular task or stage may move on when that's completed, but that's to allow you to move on too, knowing you've healed that part of your life.

This reminds me of a time during my Reiki master initiation when an angel came through to me and told me that he would be working with me on Reiki energy from now on. It was a surreal experience, but different angels come to us as we grow spiritually and become more aware.

A final thought

So here we are. The end of the book. I hope you've enjoyed learning to tap into your angels and that you can harness their support and guidance in your life. What you do with this is up to you. When I started out, I dedicated every single spare moment I had to angels and psychic development. I joined a weekly meditation circle and meditated most days. I learned everything I could about the history of the archangels and if I didn't know something, I'd tune in and ask.

The same goes for today. I have a daily spiritual practice. I study *A Course in Miracles*, practise yoga and read my own angel cards every day. My life is angels and it's a beautiful life.

Take angels with you wherever you go. They'll be with you whatever you do, whether you work in the corporate world or the service sector – even if you're a chef! Angels don't want to make you into a crazy tree-hugger, but they do want you to be connected to who you are and to live a life filled with love. Let them be your guides so that you can enjoy this journey.

As *A Course in Miracles* says, 'Teach only love, for that is what you are.'

You have my love and blessings!

Resources

Books

Angel Inspiration, Diana Cooper (Hodder & Stoughton, 2004). This is the book I had the auspicious experience with. I lay in bed looking for hope and a single white feather fell from the book.

A New Light on Angels, Diana Cooper (Findhorn Press, 2009). The revised and updated version of *A Little Light on Angels*, the first ever angel book I read.

The Big Book of Angels, Wendy Schuman (Hinkler Books, 2003). I found this book in a second hand store and it is without doubt my favourite book on angels. It shares a collection of stories from people of all walks of life – rabbis, priests, preachers and more, including Doreen Virtue.

The Lightworkers Way, Doreen Virtue (Hay House, 2004). Doreen's spiritual journey and discovery of the angels is a powerful, inspirational and profound eye-opener to living a life of purpose. I have read this book countless times.

Angels: a very short introduction, David Albert Jones (OUP Oxford; reprint edition 2011). I love this little book about the theory and history of angels. Definitely a good one if you want more scholarly information.

Archangels and Ascended Masters, Doreen Virtue (Hay House, 2004). This book is the who's who of heaven – great for therapists and to keep close by if you work professionally with angels.

Crystal Healing, Simon Lilly (element, 2002). One of my first ever spiritual books, and one that I go back to time and time again. Wanting to raise your vibration and balance your energy? Learn the basics of crystals.

Developing Mediumship, Gordon Smith (Hay House, 2009). Personally speaking I'd say Gordon Smith is the most evidential medium out there. His tips and guidance is a treasure to any sensitive wishing to develop.

Card and Oracle Decks

Healing with the Angels Oracle Cards, Doreen Virtue (Hay House, 2004)

These are the cards I use professionally every day – they're my favourite.

Angels of Light Cards, Diana Cooper (Findhorn Press, 2009)

My first ever card deck – they have become lifelong companions. I never travel anywhere without these in my backpack.

Acknowledgements

Special thanks to my mum, Diane Gray, who holds my whole life together. She's the angelic backbone in my life. Without her I would be nothing; she has held the space for me to grow, become who I am today and share it with the world. And not only does she do that, she runs my business for me – all I do is turn up. Thank you, Mum. I love you! You're the best.

I'd also like to send my appreciation to my dad, David Gray, for supporting my path and for believing in it.

Thank you to Hay House for giving me the opportunity to live my dream and to share it with the world. I am so blessed. Carolyn Thorne, Jo Burgess and Michelle Pilley, you are a dream team of lightworkers, making way for people like me and giving us a platform to share our message.

Thanks to Ruth Tewkesbury, too, for keeping me in the media and for being patient with my replies via e-mail. I'm grateful and you're a shining star.

I'd also like to send my gratitude to Robert and Hollie Holden, who have become deeply appreciated friends, to Greta Lipp for helping me grow in Europe and for being super fun, and to David Hamilton and my friend Diane Etherson, who are my soul family.

Love and support to all my friends – believe in your dreams and make them real.

Index